Aunt Phil's Trunk

Student Workbook

Bringing Alaska's history alive!

By
Laurel Downing Bill

Special credit and much appreciation to Nicole Cruz for her diligent efforts to create the best student workbook and teacher guide available for Alaska history studies.

Aunt Phil's Trunk LLC, Anchorage, Alaska
www.auntphilstrunk.com

Copyright © 2017 by Laurel Downing Bill.

All rights reserved. No part of this book may be used or reproduced in any manner whatsoever without written permission from the author, except in the case of brief quotations embodied in critical articles and reviews.

International Standard Book Number 978-1-940479-32-3
Printed and bound in the United States of America.

First Printing 2017
First Printing Second Edition 2017
First Printing Third Edition 2018

Photo credits on the front cover, from top left: Native shaman with totem, Alaska State Library, Case and Draper Collection, ASL-P-39-782; Eskimo boy, Alaska State Library, Skinner Foundation, ASL-P44-11-002; Prospector, Alaska State Library, Skinner Foundation, ASL-P44-03-15; Athabascan woman, Anchorage Museum of History and Art, Crary–Henderson Collection, AMHA-b62-1-571; Gold miners, Alaska State Library, Harry T. Becker Collection, ASL-P67-052; Chilkoot Pass, Alaska State Library, Eric A. Hegg Collection, ASL-P124-04; Seal hunter, Alaska State Library, George A. Parks Collection, ASL-P240-210; Women mending boat, Alaska State Library, Rev. Samuel Spriggs Collection, ASL-P320-60; Students in class, Alaska State Library, Wickersham State Historical Site, ASL-P277-015-029.

TABLE OF CONTENTS

Instructions *Aunt Phil's Trunk* Alaska History Curriculum 5
How to use this workbook at home 6
How to use this workbook for high school 7
How to use this workbook in the classroom 8
How to grade assignments 9
Rubric for Essay Questions 11
Rubric for Oral Presentations 12
Rubric for Enrichment Activities 12

UNIT 1: EARLY ALASKA
Lesson 1: Unanswered Questions 13
Lesson 2: Coping with the Unknown 15
Lesson 3: Explorers Ply Alaska Waters 18
Lesson 4: While the United States was Forming 22
Lesson 5: Island of Mystery 24
Lesson 6: Earthquakes Form Landscape 24
Review Lessons 1-6 26
Unit 1 Test 30

UNIT 2: LITTLE-KNOWN STORIES
Lesson 7: Natives Attack Russian Forts 32
Lesson 8: Woody Island's Icy Past 34
Lesson 9: Last Shot of the Civil War 36
Review Lessons 7-9 38
Unit 2 Test 44

UNIT 3: ALASKA BECOMES U.S. POSSESSION
Lesson 10: Seward's Folly Turns into Treasure 46
Lesson 11: Myth Surrounds Alaska Purchase 49
Lesson 12: Americans Flock North 51
Lesson 13: Apostle to the North 56
Lesson 14: Alaska's Mysterious Census-Taker 59
Review Lessons 10-14 62
Unit 3 Test 66

UNIT 4: ALASKA'S FIRST GOLD RUSH
Lesson 15: Gold Found in Southeast 68
Lesson 16: Exploring the Nile of Alaska 71
Lesson 17: Old John Bremner 76

Table of Contents

    Lesson 18: Rich Names Along the Koyukuk   78
    Review Lessons 15-18   81
    Unit 4 Test   84

UNIT 5: DREAMS OF GOLD
    Lesson 19: Alaska's Second Gold Rush   86
    Lesson 20: Dreams of Salmon Turn to Gold   88
    Lesson 21: Luckiest Man on the Klondike   91
    Review Lessons 19-21   93
    Unit 5 Test   96

UNIT 6: RUSH TO THE KLONDIKE
    Lesson 22: Dawson is Born   100
    Lesson 23: St. Michael Awakens   102
    Lesson 24: Trails to Gold   106
    Lesson 25: Gold Rush Trails Photo Essay   108
    Lesson 26: Jack Dalton Builds Toll Road   110
    Review Lessons 22-26   112
    Unit 6 Test   116

UNIT 7: SEA CAPTAINS, SCOUNDRELS AND NUNS
    Lesson 27: Sea Captain Stifles Mutiny   121
    Lesson 28: Soapy Smith Heads to Skagway   123
    Lesson 29: Miners Stampede to Nome   126
    Lesson 30: Sisters of Providence Head to Nome   128

UNIT 8: NATIVES AND THE RUSH FOR GOLD
    Lesson 31: Natives and the Rush for Gold   131
    Lesson 32: Richest Native Woman in the North   134
    Review Lessons 27-32   136
    Unit 7-8 Test   140

Extra paper for lessons   142-152

Welcome to *Aunt Phil's Trunk Volume One* Workbook for Students!

Read the chapters associated with each Unit. Then complete the lessons for that Unit to get a better understanding of Alaska's people and the events that helped shape Alaska's future.

I hope you enjoy your journey into Alaska's past from the arrival of the Native people up to around the year 1900.

Laurel Downing Bill, author

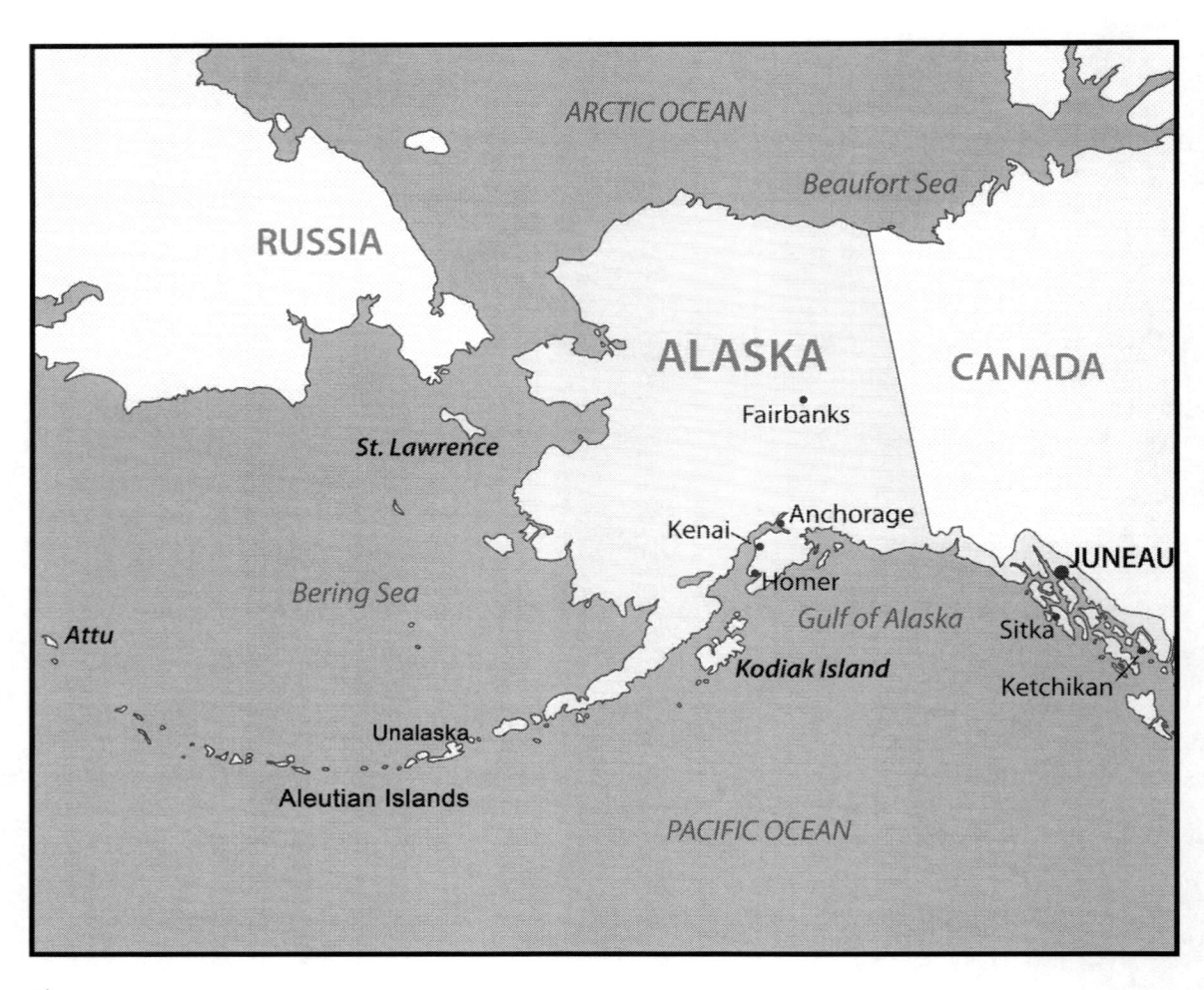

Instructions for using the *Aunt Phil's Trunk* Alaska History Curriculum

The *Aunt Phil's Trunk* Alaska History Curriculum is designed to be used in grades 4-8. High school students can use this curriculum, also, by taking advantage of the essay and enrichment activities throughout the book. The next few pages give further instruction on how to use this curriculum with middle school students, high school students and in classroom settings.

This curriculum can be taught in multiple grade levels by having your older students complete all reading, study guide work and enrichment activities independently. Students of all grade levels can participate in daily oral review by playing games like Jeopardy or Around the World.

This curriculum was developed so that students not only learn about Alaska's past, but they will have fun in the process. After every few lessons, they can test their knowledge through word scramble, word search and crossword puzzles.

Notes for parents with younger students:

1) Spiritual themes
The first chapters of this series contain detailed information about the spiritual beliefs of the Native people of Alaska. Alaska Native tribes are an important part of Alaska history and their spiritual beliefs greatly influenced their way of life. If you have concerns about introducing your child/children to spiritual topics that may vary greatly from your own family's beliefs, we encourage you to read over the chapters before your child so you can be ready to explain the belief system of early Native Alaskans, which in many cases was similar to those of indigenous people around the world.

2) Mature themes
Chapter 22 contains references to "good-time girls" during the gold rush. Parents of younger students may want to read through the chapter before your child/children and prepare yourself for any questions that may arise about these women.

How to use this workbook at home

Aunt Phil's Trunk Alaska History Curriculum is designed to be used in grades 4-8. High school students can use this curriculum, also, by taking advantage of the essay and enrichment activities throughout the book. The next page gives further instruction on how to use this curriculum with high school students.

This curriculum can be taught in multiple grade levels by having your older students complete all reading, study guide work and enrichment activities independently. Students of all grade levels can participate in daily oral review by playing games like Jeopardy or Around the World.

For Middle School Students:

1. **Facts to Know:** Read this section in the study guide with your student(s) before reading the chapter to get familiar with new terms that they will encounter in the reading.

2. **Read the chapter:** Read one chapter aloud to your student(s) or have them read it aloud to you. Older students may want to read independently.

3. **Comprehension Questions**: Younger students may answer the comprehension questions orally or write down their answers in the study guide. Use these questions to test your student(s) comprehension of the chapter. Older students should answer all questions in written form.

4. **Discussion Questions**: Have your student(s) answer these questions in a few sentences orally. Come up with follow-up questions to test your student(s) understanding of the material. Older students may answer discussion questions in written essay form.

5. **Map Work:** Some chapters will contain a map activity for your student(s) to learn more about the geography of the region that they are learning about.

6. **Enrichment and Online References:** (Optional) Assign enrichment activities as you see fit. Many of the online references are from the Alaska Humanities Forum website (http://www.akhistorycourse.org). We highly recommend this website for additional information, project ideas, etc.

7. **Unit Review:** At the end of a unit, your student will complete Unit Review questions and word puzzles in the study guide. Students should review all the chapters in the unit before completing the review. Parents may want to assist younger students with the word puzzles.

8. **Unit Test:** (Optional) There is an optional test that you can administer to your student(s) after they have completed all the unit work.

How to use this workbook for high school

1. **Facts to Know:** Your student(s) should read this section in the study guide before reading the chapter to get familiar with new terms that they will encounter.

2. **Read the chapter:** Your student(s) can read aloud or independently.

3. **Comprehension Questions:** Use these questions to test your student(s) comprehension of the chapter. Have your high schoolers write out their answers in complete sentences.

4. **Discussion Questions:** Have your student(s) answer these questions in a few sentences orally or write out their answer in essay form.

5. **Map Work:** Some chapters will contain a map activity for your student(s) to learn more about the geography of the region that they are learning about.

6. **Enrichment and Online References**: Once your high schooler has completed all the reading and study guide material for the chapter, assign additional reading from the enrichment material using the online links or book lists. Encourage your student(s) to explore topics of interest to them.

Many of the online references are from the Alaska Humanities Forum website. We highly recommend this website for additional information, project ideas, etc.

7. **Unit Review:** At the end of a unit, your student will complete Unit Review questions and word puzzles in their study guide. Students should review all the chapters in the unit before completing the review.

8. **Unit Test:** (Optional) There is an optional test that you can administer to your student(s) after they have completed all the unit work.

9. **Oral Presentation:** (Optional) Assign a 5-minute oral presentation on any topic in the reading. Encourage your student(s) to utilize the additional books and online resources to supplement the information in the textbook. Set aside a classroom day for your student(s) to share their presentations.

10. **Historical Inquiry Project:** Your student(s) will choose a topic from the reading to learn more about and explore that topic through library visits, museum trips, visiting historical sites, etc.

Visit https://www.nhd.org/how-enter-contest for detailed information on how to put together a historical inquiry project. You may even want to have your students enter the national contest.

How to use this workbook in the classroom

Aunt Phil's Trunk Alaska History Curriculum was created for homeschooling families, but it also can work well in a co-op or classroom setting. Here are some suggestions on how to use this curriculum in a classroom setting. Use what works best for your classroom.

1. **Facts to Know:** The teacher introduces students to the Facts to Know to familiarize the students with terms that they will encounter in the chapter.

2. **Read the chapter:** The teacher can read the chapter aloud while the students follow along in the book. Students also may take turns reading aloud.

3. **Comprehension Questions:** The teacher uses these questions to test the students' comprehension of the chapter. Students should write out the answers in their study guide and the teacher can review the answers with the students in class.

4. **Discussion Questions:** The teacher chooses a few students to answer these questions orally during class. Alternatively, teachers can assign these questions to be completed in essay form individually and answers can be shared during class.

5. **Map Work:** Some chapters will contain a map activity for your students to learn more about the geography of the region that they are learning about. Have your students complete the activity independently.

6. **Enrichment and Online References:** Assign enrichment activities as you see fit.

7. **Daily Review:** Students should review the material for the current unit daily. You can do this by asking review questions orally. Playing review games like Jeopardy or Around the World is a fun way to get your students excited about the material.

8. **Unit Review:** At the end of a unit, your student will complete Unit Review questions and word puzzles in the study guide. Have students review all the unit chapters before completing.

9. **Unit Test:** (Optional) There is an optional test that you can administer to your students after they have completed all the unit work.

10. **Oral Presentation:** (Optional) Assign a 5-minute oral presentation on any topic in the reading. Encourage your student(s) to utilize the additional books and online resources to supplement the information in the textbook. Set aside a classroom day for students to share their presentations.

11. **Historical Inquiry Project:** Your student(s) will choose a topic from the reading to learn more about and explore that topic through library visits, museum trips, visiting historical sites, etc.

Visit https://www.nhd.org/how-enter-contest for detailed information on how to put together a historical inquiry project. You may even want to have your students enter the national contest.

How to grade the assignments

Our rubric grids are designed to make it easy for you to grade your students' essays, oral presentations and enrichment activities. Encourage your students to look at the rubric grid before completing an assignment as a reminder of what an exemplary assignment should include.

You can mark grades for review questions, essay tests and extra credit assignments on the last page of each unit in the student workbook. Use these pages as a tool to help your students track their progress and improve their assignment grades.

Unit Review Questions

Students are given one point for each correct review and fill-in-the-blank question. Mark these points on the last page of each unit in the student workbook.

Essay Test Questions

Students will complete two or more essay questions at the end of each unit. These questions are designed to test your students' knowledge about the key topics of each unit. You can give a student up to 20 points for each essay.

Students are graded on a scale of 1-5 in four categories:

1) Understanding the topic
2) Answering all questions completely and accurately
3) Neatness and organization
4) Grammar, spelling and punctuation

Use the essay rubric grid on page 11 as a guide to give up to 5 points in each category for every essay. Mark these points for each essay on the last page of each Unit Review in the student workbook.

Word Puzzles

Word puzzles that appear at the end of the Unit Reviews count for 5 points, or you can give partial points if the student does not fill in the puzzle completely. Mark these points under the extra category on the last page of each Unit Review in the student workbook.

Enrichment Activities

Most lessons contain an enrichment activity for further research and interaction with the information in the lesson. You can make these optional or assign every activity as part of the lesson. You can use the provided rubric on page 12 to give up to 5 points for each assignment. Mark these points under the extra category on the last page of each Unit Review in the student workbook.

Oral Presentations

You have the option of assigning oral presentations on any topic from the unit as extra credit. If you choose to assign oral presentations, you can use the provided rubric to grade your student on content and presentation skills. Discuss what presentation skills you will be grading your student on before each presentation day.

Some examples of presentation skills you can grade on include:

- Eye contact with the audience
- Proper speaking volume
- Using correct posture
- Speaking clearly

Use the oral presentation rubric grid on page 12 as a guide to give up to 10 points. Mark these points under the extra category on the last page of each Unit Review in the student workbook.

Rubric for Essay Questions

	Beginning 1	Needs Improvement 2	Acceptable 3	Accomplished 4	Exemplary 5
Demonstrates Understanding of the topic	Student's work shows incomplete understanding of the topic	Student's work shows slight understanding of the topic	Student's work shows a basic understanding of the topic	Student's work shows complete understanding of the topic	Student's work demonstrates strong insight about the topic
Answered questions completely and accurately	Student's work did not address all of the questions	Student answered all of the questions with some accuracy	Student answered all questions with close to 100% accuracy	Student answered all questions with 100% accuracy	Student goes beyond the questions to demonstrate knowledge of the topic
Essay is neat and well organized	Student's work is sloppy and unorganized	Student's work is somewhat neat and organized	Student's essay is neat and somewhat organized	Student's work is well organized and neat	Student demonstrates extra care in organizing the essay and making it neat
Essay contains good grammar and spelling	Student's work is poorly written and hard to understand	Student's work contains some grammar, spelling and punctuation mistakes, but not enough to impede understanding	Student's work contains only 1 or 2 grammar, spelling or punctuation errors	Student's work contains no grammar, spelling or punctuation errors	Student's work is extremely well-written

Rubric for Oral Presentations

	Beginning 1	Needs Improvement 2	Acceptable 3	Accomplished 4	Exemplary 5
Preparation	Student did not prepare for the presentation	Student was somewhat prepared for the presentation	Student was prepared for the presentation and addressed the topic	Student was well-prepared for the presentation and addressed important points about the topic	Student prepared an excellent presentation that exhibited creativity and originality
Presentation Skills	Student demonstrated poor presentation skills (no eye contact, low volume, appears disinterested in the topic)	Student made some effort to demonstrate presentation skills (eye contact, spoke clearly, engaged audience, etc.)	Student demonstrated acceptable presentation skills (eye contact, spoke clearly, engaged audience, etc.)	Student demonstrated good presentation skills (eye contact, spoke clearly, engaged audience, etc.)	Student demonstrated strong presentation skills (eye contact, spoke clearly, engaged audience, etc.)

Rubric for Enrichment Activities

	Beginning 1	Needs Improvement 2	Acceptable 3	Accomplished 4	Exemplary 5
	Student's work is incomplete or inaccurate	Student's work is complete and somewhat inaccurate	Student completed the assignment with accuracy	Student's work is accurate, complete, neat and well-organized	Student demonstrates exceptional creativity or originality

UNIT 1: EARLY ALASKA

LESSON 1: UNANSWERED QUESTIONS

FACTS TO KNOW

Phyllis Downing Carlson (Aunt Phil) – Writer and Alaska historian whose research inspired this Alaska history book series

Cook Inlet – Area that stretches from the Gulf of Alaska to Anchorage

Petroglyph – Greek for rock carving

Potlatch – A ceremonial feast where possessions are given away to display wealth or enhance prestige

COMPREHENSION QUESTIONS

1) According to archaeologist Frederica de Laguna, how far back does the ancient Eskimo period go in the Kachemak Bay area? What does she call the phases of Eskimo history in this region?

2) Many archeologists and historians have had theories about how long the Tanaina (later called Dena'ina) people were present on the Inlet. What are two of these theories?

3) What was the significance of the stones on the Russian River to the Tanaina, according to the Natives at Kenai?

4) Why did the Native people of the Cook Inlet region fight against the Russian settlers?

5) What is the significance of Alaska's petroglyphs? What can they tell us about the Native people of Alaska?
___
___
___

DISCUSSION QUESTION

(Discuss this question with your teacher or write your answer in essay form below. Use additional paper if necessary.)

Describe what happened in the "last Indian war in Tyonek."
___
___
___
___
___
___
___
___
___
___
___
___

ENRICHMENT ACTIVITY

The Cook Inlet area that we are studying about is in Southcentral Alaska. Learn more about this region by visiting http://www.akhistorycourse.org/geography/alaskas-location and write a paragraph about what you learned.

TO LEARN MORE

Look for these books at your local library:
The First Americans: Origins, Affinities, and Adaptions. By Laughlin, William S. and Albert B. Harper New York: Gustav Fischer, 1979.

Ancient Men of the Arctic. By Giddings, J.L. New York: Alfred A. Knopf, 1967.
Eskimo Prehistory. By Bandi, Hans-George. Ann E. Keep, translator. College: University of Alaska Press, 1969.

UNIT 1: EARLY ALASKA

LESSON 2: COPING WITH THE UNKNOWN

FACTS TO KNOW

Intermediary – A person who goes between people, groups or entities
Shaman – Medicine man
Sha-E-Dah-Kla – Thought to be the most powerful medicine man in Cook Inlet

COMPREHENSION QUESTIONS

1) _____ is believed to be the birthplace of shamanism. Shamans acted as intermediaries between _____ and _____.

2) What and when was "Kiyesvilavic"? What happens during the shaman contests?
_____
_____
_____

3) What was the shaman's role in a war party? _____
_____
_____

4) In healing, the shaman seems to have acted as both _____ and _____.

5) What were the two primary causes of illness recognized by Northern Alaska Eskimo societies?
_____
_____
_____

6) What were some of the ways that shamans would heal disease or injury? _____

_____
_____
_____

DISCUSSION QUESTION

(Discuss this question with your teacher or write your answer in essay form below. Use additional paper if necessary.)

Many of the ideas that Alaska Natives had about the causes of disease and methods of healing are different from modern-day medicine. Explain how they differ using what you read in the chapter and what you know about modern-day medicine in America.

_____
_____
_____
_____
_____
_____
_____
_____
_____
_____
_____

ENRICHMENT ACTIVITY

Much of Chapter 2 was based on miraculous stories that have been passed down for generations. What is one story that has been passed down in your family? Do you have a story about an older relative that may have been passed down from your grandparents or parents? If not, ask one of your relatives for a story. Write down your story in paragraph form.

TO LEARN MORE

You can read more about shamanism by visiting http://www.akhistorycourse.org/alaskas-cultures/shamanism-a-personal-view

You can read more about traditional Native Alaskan remedies and health by visiting http://www.akhistorycourse.org/alaskas-cultures/alaska-natives-and-health

Above: A shaman's rattle, like the one seen here, was used to summon animal and ancestors' spirits to help with healing, sources say.

Below: Tlingit shaman, dressed in hide tunic with mother of pearl buttons, holds a rattle while he kneels by a sick man in the 1800s.

UNIT 1: EARLY ALASKA

LESSON 3: EXPLORERS PLY ALASKA WATERS

FACTS TO KNOW

Vitus Bering – Danish-born explorer for the Russian Navy/Bering Sea was named after him
Northwest Passage – A fabled trading route across the top of North America from Europe to Asia
Aleuts – Native Alaskan group mainly residing in south and southwest Alaska
Captain James Cook – English explorer who searched for the Northwest Passage

COMPREHENSION QUESTIONS

1) When did European explorers first start coming to Alaska? Who did they find there?
_____
_____
_____

2) In 1728, Danish-born navigator _____, sailing for the _____ Navy of Czar Peter the Great, made his way through the narrow waterway that separates the Seward Peninsula of Alaska from the Chukotka Peninsula to Siberia. What happened during his first voyage? And his second?
_____
_____
_____

3) How did the Russian traders treat the Aleut people? _____
_____
_____
_____

4) Russia was not the only country to send explorers to Alaska. The _____, _____, and _____ governments also were eager to share in Alaska's bounty.

5) When did Captain James Cook sail to Alaska? What was he looking for? What important discoveries did he make?

_____
_____
_____

DISCUSSION QUESTION

(Discuss this question with your teacher or write your answer in essay form below. Use additional paper if necessary.)

We learned that explorers came to Alaska from all over the world. What were some of the reasons that the explorers came to Alaska?

MAP ACTIVITY

When Europeans began exploring Alaska in the early 18th-century, they found the land already inhabited by various Native groups. Using the map below and Page 29 in your textbook, write down the name of the Native group the Europeans encountered in each region.

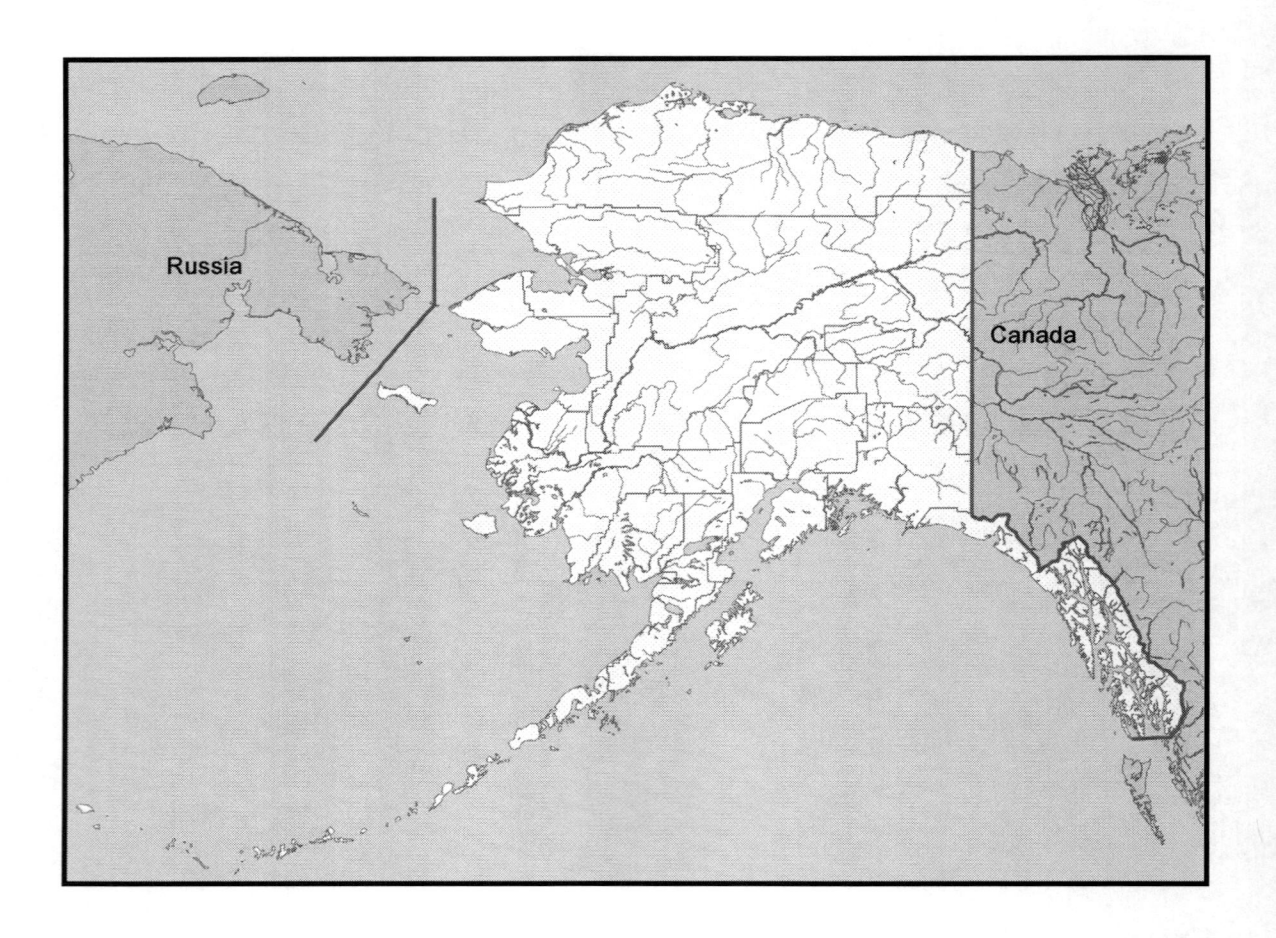

Early Alaska History
Word Scramble

Please unscramble the words below

1. trftasiac   Objects made by a human being, typically an item of cultural or historical interest.

2. heiCf   A leader or ruler of a people or clan.

3. naSahm   A person regarded as having access to, and influence in, the world of good and evil spirits.

4. ahptoclt   A ceremonial feast at which possessions are given away to display wealth or enhance prestige.

5. mttneeltse   A place, typically one that previously has been uninhabited, where people establish a community.

6. uiamk   An Eskimo open boat made with skin stretched over a wooden frame.

7. drtaun   A vast, flat and treeless Arctic region in which the subsoil is permanently frozen.

8. ucrtelu   The way of life, especially the general customs and beliefs, of a particular group of people.

9. ecldsanap   All the visible features of an area of countryside or land.

10. ogltpepyhr   A carving or inscription on a rock.

UNIT 1: EARLY ALASKA

LESSON 4: WHILE THE UNITED STATES WAS FORMING

FACTS TO KNOW

Juan Perez – Spanish explorer who discovered Mount Edgecumbe and Shelikof Bay
Russian-American Company – Government sponsored company that monopolized the fur-trading industry in Alaska
Alexander Andreevich Baranof – First manager of the Russian-American Company

COMPREHENSION QUESTIONS

For each United States historical event, list which important event was happening in Alaska at or around that time:

1) The Revolutionary War (1775) _____

2) The Second Continental Congress adopted the Declaration of Independence (1776)

3) Eight days after the signing of the Declaration of Independence

4) The Philadelphia Convention was drawing up the Constitution (1776-1781)

5) After the defeat of the English at Yorktown and the Articles of Confederation (1781-1783)

DISCUSSION QUESTION

(Discuss this question with your teacher or write your answer in essay form below. Use additional paper if necessary.)

From Page 39, "So while the United States was struggling to become a nation after throwing off the yoke of colonialism, Alaska, which later became its northernmost state, was being explored, exploited, and taken over by western nations. Its colonization of the United States was coming to an end."

Explain this quote in your own words. Then share two examples from the chapter to back up this statement.

_____
_____
_____
_____
_____
_____
_____
_____
_____
_____
_____
_____
_____
_____
_____
_____
_____

ENRICHMENT ACTIVITY

Imagine that you are an explorer to Alaska from a distant land. Write your own log entry (journal) about one of your adventures in exploration. What did you see? Who did you meet? What happened?

TO LEARN MORE

You can read more about the Russian explorers to Alaska by visiting http://www.akhistorycourse.org/russias-colony/alaskas-heritage/chapter-3-1-russians-come-to-alaska

You can read more about the beginning of exploration in Alaska by visiting http://www.akhistorycourse.org/russias-colony/the-beginning-of-exploration

UNIT 1: EARLY ALASKA

LESSON 5: ISLAND OF MYSTERY
LESSON 6: EARTHQUAKES FORM LANDSCAPE

Note: Read both chapters 5 and 6 before completing this lesson.

FACTS TO KNOW

Bogoslof – Island created by volcanic activity west of Unalaska/Dutch Harbor
Earthquake – A sudden and violent shaking of the ground, sometimes causing great destruction, as a result of movements within the earth's crust or volcanic action
Landscape – All the visible features of an area of countryside or land

COMPREHENSION QUESTIONS

1) What is the name of the "island of mystery" described in Chapter 5? Why is it called the island of mystery? _____
_____
_____

2) Describe the emergence of Castle Rock in 1796.
_____
_____
_____

3) Name some animals Lt. George E. Morris Jr. found living on Bogoslof in the 1930s?
_____
_____
_____

4) On what parts of Alaska's landscape can you see evidence of earthquakes?
_____
_____
_____
_____

5) Southeast Alaska experienced a series of major earthquakes, including one that threatened to wipe out which town on April 2, 1836? What annual tradition did Bishop Veniaminov institute after this earthquake?

_____
_____
_____

6) At _____ Bay there is a great "loose joint" in the earth's crust, geologists say. Some of the world's mightiest _____ and _____ lie astride it, and when _____ occur mountains twist, shake and tumble around.

7) Uplift and subsidence that accompanied the _____ earthquake in _____ affected an area of at least 34,000 square miles.

DISCUSSION QUESTION

(Discuss this question with your teacher or write your answer in essay form below. Use additional paper if necessary.)

After reading Chapters 5 and 6, why do you think the earthquakes and volcanic eruptions that we studied are an important part of Alaska's history?

_____
_____
_____
_____
_____
_____
_____
_____
_____
_____
_____
_____

TO LEARN MORE

You can read more about why the geological history of Alaska is so important by visiting http://www.akhistorycourse.org/geography/alaskas-heritage/chapter-1-1-geological-and-glacial-history

TIME TO REVIEW

Review Chapters 1-6 of your book before moving on to the Unit Review. See how many questions you can answer without looking at your book.

UNIT 1: EARLY ALASKA

REVIEW LESSONS 1-6

Write down what you remember about:

Phyllis Downing Carlson (Aunt Phil) _____

Cook Inlet _____

Potlatch _____

Shaman _____

Petroglyphs _____

Intermediary _____

Vitus Bering _____

Northwest Passage _____

Aleuts _____

Captain James Cook _____

Russian-American Company _____

Bogoslof _____

Earthquake _____

Landscape _____

Fill in the blanks:

1) _____, a dedicated archaeologist who carried out a thorough study of the ancient Eskimo culture in the _____ Bay during the 1930s divided the Eskimo culture in _____ Bay into three stages that she called _____.

2) Joan Townsend places the beginning of Tanaina (Dena'ina) occupancy around _____ years _____ the coming of the Russians in the last quarter of the 18th-century. When Captain James Cook, in _____, described the people he met in what is today known as Cook Inlet, they and their culture strongly resembled some late descriptions of the Tanaina.

3) It was reported by the Natives at Kenai that stones on the Russian River acted as _____ when the Tanaina were attacked by the _____. Nickafor Alexan, one of the oldtimers at the Indian village Tyonek on the west side of _____, told Aunt Phil of the last Indian War in his village. It was between the _____ and _____ people.

4) Alaska's _____, Greek for rock carving, are among many enigmas of science. The carvings are in Southeastern Alaska and are unique because they are associated with _____, rather than primitive village sites, and always face the sea.

5) _____ is believed to be the birthplace of shamanism. Shamans acted as intermediaries between _____ and _____. In healing, the _____ seems to have acted as both _____ and _____ _____.

6) When _____ explorers rounded the coasts of Alaska in the early _____ century, they discovered the country inhabited by _____ in the north, west and Prince William Sound areas; _____ in the southwest; _____ in the interior and Cook Inlet areas; and _____ and _____ Indians in the southeast.

7) In 1728, Danish-born navigator _____, sailing for the _____ Navy of Czar Peter the Great, made his way through the narrow waterway that separates the Seward Peninsula of Alaska from the Chukotka Peninsula to Siberia.

27

8) Russia was not the only country to send explorers to Alaska. The _____, _____, and _____ governments also were eager to share in Alaska's bounty.

9) Captain _____ set sail in _____ aboard his ship _____ to find the fabled _____, a trading route across the top of North America, from _____ to _____.

10) The mystery island, named _____, is composed of _____ that's unstable and shifts with the tide. Its first recorded eruption occurred in _____.

11) In _____, all heck broke lose at Yakutat and _____. At about 10:17 p.m. an _____ began to shake a vast area of Southeastern Alaska and northern British Columbia.

12) The story of Alaska's _____ is written in our _____. The evidence attests to _____ awesome power.

28

Early Alaska History
Word Search
Please find the words below

```
                        E
                        T
                     O  A  V
                     S  R  O
                  S  F  G  T  H
                  Y  N  I  R  L
               T  G  O  M  A  Q  O
               T  O  M  F  P  J  E
S  N  D  U  W  R  P  A  L  A  S  S  N  S  Y  K  A  Y  A  K  F
   T  Z  T  D  W  I  R  O  D  D  G  A  U  H  R  B  P  R  Z
      E  C  R  I  Q  U  E  I  U  F  M  O  O  U  B  N  B
         L  A  A  G  R  A  C  E  R  A  H  S  S  H  O
            E  M  D  L  H  H  F  R  H  E  N  C  O
               C  P  E  C  F  A  M  S  K  A  O
               O  A  S  R  B  S  T  P  O  I  P
               S  F  Z  R  A  S  W  E  V  M  D  P  S
               T  V  A  R  B  Q     U  B  S  N  E  B
            Z  L  A  A  P  R           K  I  I  R  S  P
            F  E  B  N  N              X  R  J  C  R
         R  Y  P  A                       T  U  E  I
         Q  Y                                J  T
         N                                      N
```

Words

ARCHAEOLOGY	COPPER	MIGRATE	SMOKEHOUSE
BARABARA	FEUDS	NOMADIC	TRADERS
BRACELETS	INDIANS	PELTS	TRAPS
CAMPS	KAYAK	SHAMAN	TRIBES

UNIT 1: EARLY ALASKA

UNIT TEST

Choose *two* of the following questions to answer in paragraph form. Use as much detail as possible to completely answer the question. Use extra paper in back of the book if needed.

1) Aunt Phil had many unanswered questions about Alaska's history. What was one of her unanswered questions? Describe one or more theories that may answer this question.

2) Describe the impact of the Russian fur traders settling in Alaska. How did they treat the Natives? How did the Natives treat the Russians?

3) Why did explorers come to Alaska from all over the world? Give at least one example of an explorer that came to Alaska. When did he come to Alaska and why? What happened when he got to Alaska?

4) What significance did the volcanic eruptions and earthquakes have on Alaska's history? Name one of these events and describe the impact it had on the area.

Aunt Phil's Trunk Volume One

UNIT 1: EARLY ALASKA

    Review Questions   _____ (possible 14 pts.)
      Fill-the-Blanks   _____ (possible 12 pts.)

Unit Test
  Essay 1
     Demonstrates understanding of the topic   _____ (possible 5 pts.)
     Answered the questions completely and accurately   _____ (possible 5 pts.)
     Composition is neat   _____ (possible 5 pts.)
     Grammar and Spelling   _____ (possible 5 pts.)

  Essay 2
     Demonstrates understanding of the topic   _____ (possible 5 pts.)
     Answered the questions completely and accurately   _____ (possible 5 pts.)
     Composition is neat   _____ (possible 5 pts.)
     Grammar and Spelling   _____ (possible 5 pts.)

                                              Subtotal Points _____ **(possible 66 pts.)**

Extra Credit
    Word Puzzle   _____ (5 pt. per completed puzzle)
    Complete an Enrichment Activity   _____ (possible 5 pts.)
    Oral presentation   _____ (possible 10 pts.)

    Total Extra Credit   _____

                                                Total Unit Points _____

GRADE CHART

A   60-66+ points

B   53-59 points

C   46-52 points

D   39-45 points

UNIT 2: LITTLE-KNOWN STORIES

LESSON 7: NATIVES ATTACK RUSSIAN FORTS

FACTS TO KNOW

    Tlingit Indians – Members of an American Indian people of the coasts and islands of southeastern Alaska, including Sitka, and adjacent British Columbia
    Nulato – Athabascan village on the Yukon River/name means "dog salmon camp"
    Petr Malakhov – Assistant navigator for Russian-American Company who saw Nulato's trading potential
    New Archangel – Name of the Russian settlement in southeast Alaska after Alexander Baranof rebuilt it in 1804 (later known as Sitka)

COMPREHENSION QUESTIONS

1) In 1802, which group attacked the Russian settlement in Sitka while Alexander Baranof was away? Why did they attack? _____
_____
_____

2) When did Baranof return to the settlement? What did he bring with him? For what purpose?
_____
_____
_____

3) When did Nulato become a trading center for the Russians? Who noticed the trading potential of this area? Did the villagers want to trade with the Russians?
_____
_____
_____

4) For ___ years, the Russians traded peacefully with the village of _____ which means "dog salmon camp." But on a dark Sunday, February 16, _____, that all changed when the _____ came to town.

5) Describe what happened during the massacre.

6) What are some of the theories that have arisen to explain the massacre?

DISCUSSION QUESTION

(Discuss this question with your teacher or write your answer in essay form below. Use additional paper if necessary.)

In his book, *On the Edge of Nowhere*, Jimmy Huntington wrote about the trading process of his Native people. Describe this process.

ENRICHMENT ACTIVITY

Download the Russian American Reader at http://www.akhistorycourse.org/docs/russian_american_book7.pdf

Read the letters between Russia and Kodiak on pages 4-10, and then write a paragraph describing what you learned about the Russian-American Company.

TO LEARN MORE

Read more about the Russian colonization of Alaska by visiting http://www.akhistorycourse.org/docs/russian_american_book7.pdf

Look for this book at your local library:
Kodiak and Afognak Life, 1868-1870. Richard A. Pierce. Kingston, Ontario, Canada: The Limestone Press, 1981.

UNIT 2: LITTLE-KNOWN STORIES

LESSON 8: WOODY ISLAND'S ICY PAST

FACTS TO KNOW

Woody Island – Small island a couple miles off the city of Kodiak
Lake Tanignak – 40-acre lake on Woody Island
Barabara – A sod or turf hut built partly or wholly underground
Tione – Chief

COMPREHENSION QUESTIONS

1) Woody Island is a place of many of Alaska's firsts. What are some of those firsts? Why did these firsts happen here? _____
_____
_____

2) Why was Alaska a prime area for selling ice to California? What part of Alaska did the first shipment come from? How much did that shipment sell for?
_____
_____
_____

3) Between _____ and _____, more than _____ tons of ice was shipped as far south as _____ and _____, bringing at first $_____ a ton. Later the price fell to $_____ a ton as _____ increased.

4) In the early 1850s, artificial ice machines were invented, but they didn't sell very well. Why not? What did the ice machine manufacturer do to try to stifle competition?
_____
_____
_____

5) When was the end of the ice industry in Alaska? Why did it end?
_____
_____
_____

34

DISCUSSION QUESTION

(Discuss this question with your teacher or write your answer in essay form below. Use additional paper if necessary.)

Describe what life was like on Woody Island for the Native workers.

LEARN MORE

Read more about the Alaska Ice Company and other economic activities that Russians took part in by visiting http://www.akhistorycourse.org/russias-colony/alaskas-heritage/chapter-3-6-other-economic-activity

UNIT 2: LITTLE-KNOWN STORIES

LESSON 9: LAST SHOT OF THE CIVIL WAR

FACTS TO KNOW

Shenandoah – An English-built Confederate vessel used to disrupt northern commerce on the high seas

Appomattox – Place where the American Civil War ended in April 1865

Confederate – A supporter of the Confederate States of America during the American Civil War, 1861-1865.

Yankee – Slang term for a member of the United States of America by the Confederates (also refers to a person who lives in, or is from, the United States)

COMPREHENSION QUESTIONS

1) What was "the last shot of the civil war," and when did it happen?
_____
_____
_____

2) Why was the *Shenandoah* in the Bering Sea of Alaska?
_____
_____
_____

3) The Shenandoah covered _____ miles and captured _____ Yankee ships.

4) How and when did the crew of the *Shenandoah* learn the war was over? _____
_____
_____
_____

5) Where and when did the commander and crew of the *Shenandoah* surrender?
_____
_____
_____

DISCUSSION QUESTION

(Discuss this question with your teacher or write your answer in essay form below. Use additional paper if necessary.)

How do you think America would be different if the Confederates had won the Civil War?

LEARN MORE

Read more about the American Civil War, also called War Between the States, by visiting https://www.britannica.com/event/American-Civil-War

TIME TO REVIEW

Review Chapters 7-9 before moving on to the Unit Review. See how many questions you can answer without looking at your book.

UNIT 2: LITTLE-KNOWN STORIES

REVIEW LESSONS 7-9

Write down what you remember about:

Tlingit Indians _____

Petr Malakhov _____

Nulato _____

New Archangel _____

Woody Island _____

Lake Tanignak _____

Barabara _____

Tione _____

Shenandoah _____

Appomattox _____

Confederate _____

Yankee _____

Fill in the blanks:

1) In the year _____, a group of _____ warriors attacked the Russian settlement while _____ was away in Kodiak.

2) In April _____, _____ returned to Sitka with four small ships, 300 canoes, and a crew of 121 _____ and 800 _____. He retook the fort and erected a stronger stockade and buildings and renamed the settlement _____.

3) The _____ region came to the attention of the rest of the country, too, when in _____, _____ Natives destroyed the Russian fort at _____.

4) _____ an Athabascan village on the _____ River, became a trading center for the _____ when Russian-American Company assistant navigator _____, a Creole, traveled from the company's western fur depot in St. Michael up the Yukon River.

5) The _____ established on Woody Island was perhaps unique in commercial enterprises because its main product was _____, which was needed to preserve _____, something abundant in Alaska that _____ wanted.

6) Between _____ and _____, more than _____ tons of ice was shipped as far south as _____ and _____, bringing at first $____ a ton. Later the price fell to $____ a ton as _____ increased.

7) The end of the ice industry came when the _____ was built to the coast, making it feasible to ship natural ice form the Sierras into San Francisco, and when _____ was invented the price was forced too low to justify Alaska expenses.

8) Not knowing that the American Civil War had ended in Appomattox _____ days earlier, the commander of an English-built _____ vessel named _____ fired upon several whalers near _____ Island on June 22, _____.

9) After learning the war had ended, the comander and crew took the Confederate ship to _____ where they surrendered on _____.

39

Early Alaska History
Crossword Puzzle

Read Across and Down clues and fill in blank boxes that match numbers on the clues

Across
1. A ship or large boat
2. Country in which the *Shenandoah* surrendered in November 1865
4. Also known as The War Between the States
7. Supporter of the Confederate States of America during American Civil War
8. Small pieces of glass, stone or similar material used in decoration and trading
9. People who buy and sell goods
11. A brutal slaughter of people
12. Alaska Native group that attacked the Russian fort at Mikhailovsk
15. A barrier formed from upright wooden posts or stakes as a defense against attack
16. Frozen water
20. Lake where residents of Woody Island chipped ice for shipping
21. Drink that workers received every day when working at Woody Island ice business
22. Slang term for a member of the United States of America
24. The Russian settlement in Southeast Alaska called New Archangel later became known as this town
25. Woody Island had one of these to saw logs into lumber and sawdust
26. A building designed to be defended from attack
27. Animal skin, fur and all

Down
1. Small communities or groups of houses or huts in rural areas
3. Place where the American Civil War ended in April 1865
5. Village name that means "dog salmon camp"
6. A person who fights in battles and is known for having courage and skill
8. A sod or turf hut built partially or wholly underground
10. A sum of money or other payment demanded or paid for the release of a prisoner
13. A large body of ice that moves slowly and spreads outward on a land surface
14. Name of island where the residents worked in an ice business in the mid-1800s
15. Red Shirt was one of these
17. First manager of the Russian-American Company
18. The basic monetary unit of Russia
19. A narrow, keel-less boat with pointed ends, propelled by paddles
23. Another word for Chief

Early Alaska History
Crossword Puzzle

Courtesy Alaska State Library

Courtesy Alaska State Library

Fur became a hot commodity for eary fur traders in Alaska. The Native people had used animal fur and skins for clothing, shelter and other items long before Russian fur traders arrived, as seen in the photos on Page 38.

But fur, and later ice, were not the only commodities that early traders in Alaska exploited. The photo below shows how white whalers and traders cleaned pieces of baleen, a filter-feeder system inside the mouths of baleen whales, during the 1800s to ship to eager buyers in the Lower 48.

Baleen was used much as plastic is used today. Fashionable ladies wore corsets made from baleen to compress their waistlines. One typical corset advertisement from the 1800s proudly proclaimed, "Real Whalebone Only Used."

It also was used for collar stays, buggy whips and toys. Its flexibility led it to be used as the springs in early typewriters, too.

The comparison to plastic is apt. Think of common items which today might be made of plastic, and it's likely that similar items in the 1800s would have been made of whalebone.

Courtesy Alaska State Library

UNIT 2: LITTLE-KNOWN STORIES

UNIT TEST

Choose *two* of the following questions to answer in paragraph form. Use as much detail as possible to completely answer the question. Use extra paper in back of the book if needed.

1) What was the impact of Russian colonization on Alaska's history? Include specific examples.

2) Describe one of the Native attacks on Russian forts as written in Chapter 7 in as much detail as possible. Why did this attack occur?

3) Summarize "Alaska's Wackiest Industry" from start to finish. How did it start and where? What competition did it face? How did it end?

4) What was "the last shot of the civil war"? What happened? Who was involved?

Aunt Phil's Trunk Volume One

UNIT 2: LITTLE-KNOWN STORIES

  Review Questions   _____ (possible 12 pts.)
  Fill-the-Blanks   _____ (possible 9 pts.)

Unit Test
 Essay 1
  Demonstrates understanding of the topic   _____ (possible 5 pts.)
  Answered the questions completely and accurately   _____ (possible 5 pts.)
  Composition is neat   _____ (possible 5 pts.)
  Grammar and Spelling   _____ (possible 5 pts.)

 Essay 2
  Demonstrates understanding of the topic   _____ (possible 5 pts.)
  Answered the questions completely and accurately   _____ (possible 5 pts.)
  Composition is neat   _____ (possible 5 pts.)
  Grammar and Spelling   _____ (possible 5 pts.)

              Subtotal Points _____ **(possible 61 pts.)**

Extra Credit
  Word Puzzle   _____ (5 pt. per completed puzzle)
  Complete an Enrichment Activity   _____ (possible 5 pts.)
  Oral presentation   _____ (possible 10 pts.)

  Total Extra Credit   _____

              Total Unit Points _____

GRADE CHART

A 55-61+ points

B 49-54 points

C 43-48 points

D 37-42 points

UNIT 3: ALASKA BECOMES U.S. POSSESSION

LESSON 10: SEWARD'S FOLLY TURNS INTO TREASURE

FACTS TO KNOW:

William H. Seward – U.S. Secretary of State who negotiated with Russia for the purchase of Alaska

Edouard de Stoecki – Russian ambassador who negotiated with Seward to sell Alaska to America

General Jeff Davis – U.S. general that took possession of Alaska from the Russians in 1867

Sitka – The town in Southeast Alaska where the Russian governor of Alaska formally transferred ownership of Alaska to the United States

COMPREHESION QUESTIONS

1) What value did U.S. Secretary of State William H. Seward find in Alaska? _____
_____
_____
_____

2) When did America sign a treaty to purchase Alaska? What were the terms of the deal between the United States and Russia? When did the U.S. take possession of Alaska?
_____
_____
_____

3) Many Americans, including legislators, thought that it was a bad idea to purchase Alaska. Why? _____
_____
_____

4) What did the U.S. do shortly after taking possession of Alaska? How did the transfer affect Sitka? _____
_____
_____

5) What happened on April 14, 1865, that could have prevented the United States from purchasing Alaska? _____
_____
_____

DISCUSSION QUESTIONS

(Discuss this question with your teacher or write your answer in essay form below. Use additional paper if necessary.)

How did the Russian population react to the purchase of Alaska? Did they welcome the incoming Americans? How did the Native people of Alaska react?

_____
_____
_____
_____
_____
_____
_____
_____
_____
_____
_____
_____
_____
_____
_____
_____

BONUS QUESTION

What do you think would have happened to Alaska if William H. Seward had been killed by the Confederate assassin? Do you think Alaska would still be part of Russia? If so, what effect would that have had on the United States today?

ENRICHMENT ACTIVITY

U.S. Secretary of State William Seward saw the value of Alaska to the United States when many Americans did not. Imagine that you are Secretary Seward. Write a persuasive letter to one of your friends that has doubts about your reasons for wanting to purchase Alaska. Address the doubts that many Americans had about the value of Alaska.

TO LEARN MORE

Read more about the Russian sale of Alaska by visiting http://www.akhistorycourse.org/russias-colony/the-sale-of-russian-america

Look for this book at your local library:
Lady Franklin Visits Sitka, Alaska, 1870. DeArmond, R.N., editor. Anchorage: Alaska Historical Society, 1981.

The U.S. Army took over the Russian-American Company administrative office building in Sitka, seen here, once Alaska was officially transferred to America on Oct. 18, 1867.

UNIT 3: ALASKA BECOMES U.S. POSSESSION

LESSON 11: MYTH SURROUNDS ALASKA PURCHASE

FACTS TO KNOW:

Czar Alexander II – Russian leader who sent the Russian fleet to America in 1863
President Abraham Lincoln – The 16th President of the United States
American Civil War – A civil war fought from 1861-1865 between the Union and the Confederate States (southern states that seceded in order to prevent President Abraham Lincoln from outlawing slavery in their states)

COMPREHENSION QUESTIONS

1) How much did the United States pay for Alaska? Why did some people think that the purchase price was considerably less? _____

2) Was President Abraham Lincoln happy about the arrival of the Russian fleet in American during 1863? Why or why not? _____

3) Why did Britain withdraw its support for the Union? Why was neutrality on the Civil War in the best interest of Britain? Why was neutrality in the best interest of France?

4) How did New Yorkers welcome the Russian fleet on November 5, 1863? What was said about Czar Alexander II at the event? _____

5) Historical records show that the United States inquired about purchasing Alaska long before the Civil War. When were the first inquires made into purchasing Alaska and by whom? Why didn't the U.S. purchase Alaska at that point? _____
_____
_____
_____

DISCUSSION QUESTION

(Discuss this question with your teacher or write your answer in essay form below. Use additional paper if necessary.)

What two-fold purpose did Czar Alexander sending the Russian fleet to America accomplish?

_____
_____
_____
_____
_____
_____
_____
_____
_____
_____
_____
_____
_____
_____

ENRICHMENT ACTIVITY

Read this article http://www.akhistorycourse.org/governing-alaska/after-the-purchase-of-alaska and answer this question:

What did you learn about the Native people's views on the United States purchase of Alaska? Write your answer in paragraph form.

TO LEARN MORE

Read more about the American contact with Russian America by visiting http://www.akhistorycourse.org/russias-colony/alaskas-heritage/chapter-3-10-american-contact-with-russian-america

UNIT 3: ALASKA BECOMES U.S. POSSESSION

LESSON 12: AMERICANS FLOCK NORTH

FACTS TO KNOW:

Wrangell – Third-oldest community in Alaska and home of one of the first U.S. Army posts in Alaska

Unalaska – The largest town of the Aleutian islands

Census – The process of acquiring data about the members of a specific population

Russian Orthodox Church – Religious denomination of the Russians that settled in Alaska

COMPREHENSION QUESTIONS

1) Name some of the reasons that Americans were eager to go to Alaska? What area did many of them travel to? _____
_____
_____
_____

2) When _____ took the first United States Census in _____, he counted _____ people in the colony. His report provided an abundance of information about Alaska's _____ and geography.

3) When Americans arrived in Alaska, what new settlements did they establish? What industries became important as a result of these new settlements? _____
_____
_____
_____

4) What became the leading industry in Alaska after the decline of fur at the turn of the century? _____
_____
_____
_____

5) Who was Saint Innocent of Alaska? What significant things did he do in Alaska?

_____
_____
_____
_____

DISCUSSION QUESTION

(Discuss this question with your teacher or write your answer in essay form below. Use additional paper if necessary.)

As its population grew, several religious groups flooded Alaska. Name one of these groups. What Native people did this religious group serve? What important things did this group do?

_____
_____
_____
_____
_____
_____
_____
_____
_____
_____
_____
_____
_____

ENRICHMENT ACTIVITY

History is made up of numerous cause-and-effect relationships. No historical event happens in isolation. Part of historical study is learning how people, places, movements and events are interrelated. Consider what you have learned thus far about the history of Alaska. Write down five cause-and-effect relationships that you notice from your reading. Example: When the United States purchased Alaska in 1867, Americans flocked to Alaska for new economic opportunity.

TO LEARN MORE

Read more about the population and settlements of Alaska after the U.S. purchase by visiting http://www.akhistorycourse.org/americas-territory/population-and-settlements

The Sitka Home Mission, established by Presbyterian missionary Sheldon Jackson and shown above in 1886-1887, served as the education center for Alaska Native children in and around Sitka after Alaska became a U.S. possession in 1867.

The slate tablet shown below was used by a 4-year-old boy who wrote, in chalk, "The book is on the box. It is a big hat. It is my book." He also drew pictures of various items, including a goblet, which was probably a very new word in his vocabulary.

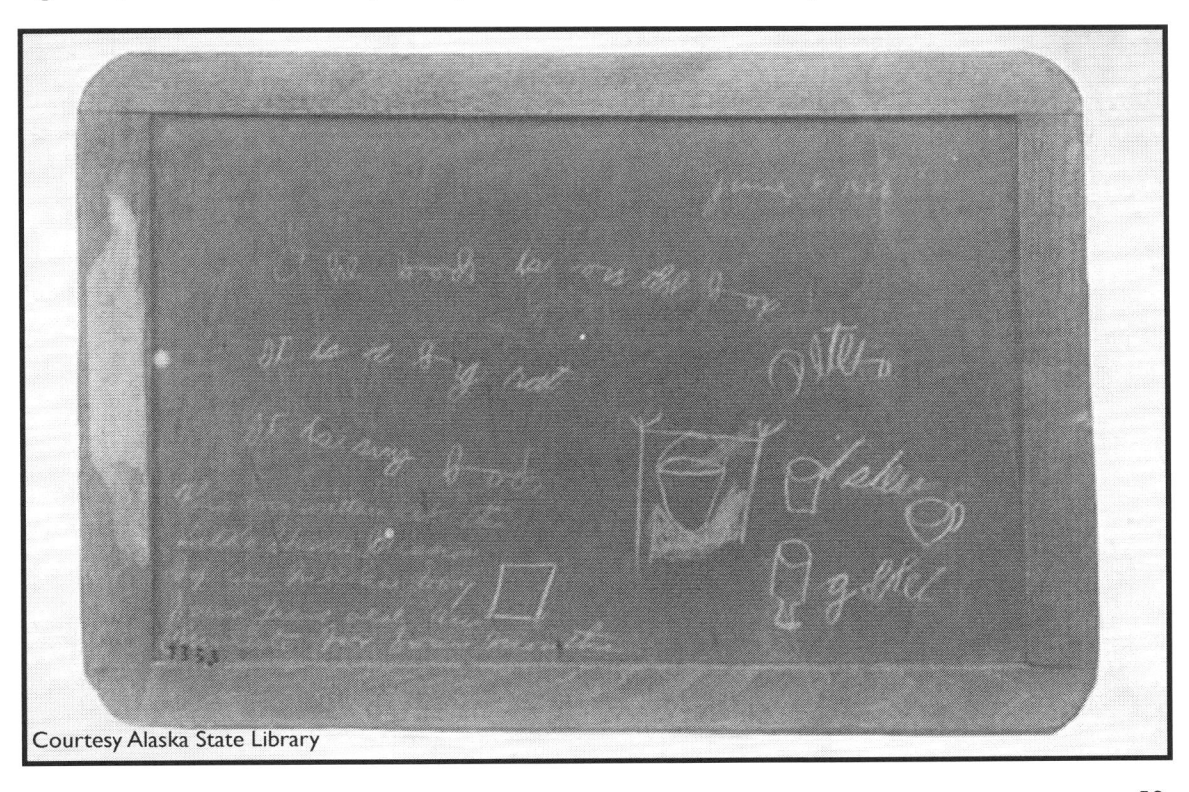

Alaska Purchase
Crossword Puzzle

Read Across and Down clues and fill in blank boxes that match numbers on the clues

Across

2 The Russian admiral who sailed the Russian fleet into New York Harbor in 1863
4 This man took possession of Alaska from the Russians in October 1867
7 Department of U.S. Government that first oversaw Alaska affairs
8 A position usable as a base for further advance
11 The action of becoming larger or more extensive
17 A person who is among the first to explore or settle a new country or area
18 An act of moving something or someone to another place
20 An item of property; something belonging to one
21 The formal giving up of rights, property or territory
22 19th-century doctrine that believed expansion of the United States was both justified and inevitable
23 A person or company involved in wholesale trade
27 Lack of good sense; foolishness
28 Russian Ambassador who brokered Alaska purchase with America
29 The state of not supporting or helping either side in a conflict
31 He took the first U.S. Census for Alaska in 1880
33 Largest town on Aleutian islands and place where the Methodist Church came in 1890
35 The man who negotiated the purchase of Alaska from the Russians
36 This village was first named Mamterillermiut, meaning "Smokehouse People"
38 When the 13 colonies that became the United States came together, they formed this
39 A card game played by William Seward, usually for two pairs of players
40 The process of acquiring data about the members of a specific population
41 The emotional or mental condition of those fighting during the American Civil War with respect to confidence and loyalty
42 The largest group of naval vessels under one commander

Down

1 Russian general who submitted contingency plan for the weak Russian navy in 1863
3 The capacity to have an effect on the character, development or behavior of something
5 A person who serves in an army
6 People sent by a church into an area to carry on evangelism or other activities
9 Man who attempted to assassinate Secretary of State Seward in 1865
10 The formal activities conducted on some solemn or important public or state occasion
12 The action of buying something
13 Third-oldest community in Alaska and home of one of Alaska's first U.S. Army posts
14 A Native who became one of the most influential and capable missionaries in Alaska
15 A person from the same country or region as someone else
16 Place in Sitka where the official transfer of Alaska to America occurred
19 A person who unlawfully occupies an uninhabited building or unused land
24 U.S. President at the time of Alaska purchase from Russia
25 Forecast an uncertain event

Alaska Purchase
Crossword Puzzle

Down (continued)
26 Chief of Klukwan who gave William H. Seward a special blanket when Seward visited southeast Alaska after the Alaska purchase.
30 A formally concluded and ratified agreement between countries
32 This became the leading industry in Alaska as the fur industry declined
34 U.S. Senator who supported Alaska purchase
36 Type of knife the would-be assassin used when attacking Secretary of State Seward
37 Place where ceremony to transfer Alaska to Russia was held
41 A widely held but false belief or idea

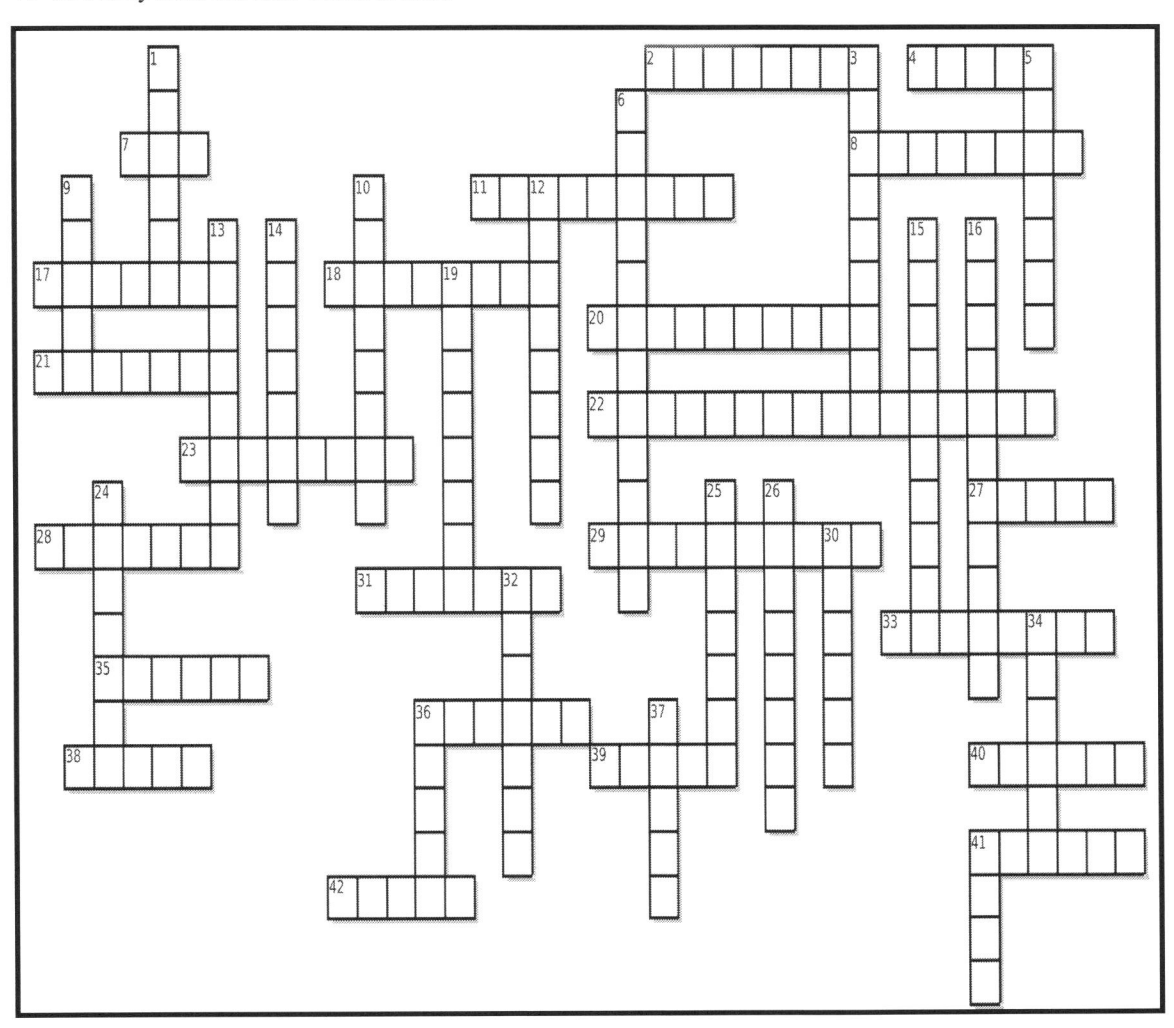

55

UNIT 3: ALASKA BECOMES U.S. POSSESSION

LESSON 13: APOSTLE TO THE NORTH

FACTS TO KNOW:

Fort Yukon – A trading post established by Alexander Murray
William Carpenter Bompas – English missionary and teacher in the Yukon
Miner – A person who extracts ore, coal or other minerals from the earth
George Washington Carmack – One of the men who discovered gold along Rabbit Creek, later named Bonanza, that started the Klondike Gold Rush

COMPREHENSION QUESTIONS

1) How did William Carpenter Bompas begin his mission to the Yukon?
_____
_____
_____

2) After leaving London in 1865, how long did it take William Carpenter Bompas to relieve Rev. McDonald of his post in the Yukon? What did he do during that time?
_____
_____
_____

3) Describe Bishop Bompas' wife.
_____
_____
_____

4) Why was Fort Yukon described as, "a half mile from the ends of the earth"?
_____
_____
_____

5) What important discovery was made on the banks of the Klondike River in 1896?
_____
_____
_____

DISCUSSION QUESTION

(Discuss this question with your teacher or write your answer in essay form below. Use additional paper if necessary.)

Bishop Bompas and Reverend McDonald spent a lot of time studying the languages of the Native people. Reverend McDonald required his new clergy to spend at least four hours a day in language study. Why was this important? What do you think this meant to the Native people that they served?

TO LEARN MORE

Read more about the Yukon River and its people by visiting http://www.akhistorycourse.org/interior-alaska/the-yukon-river-and-its-people

MAP ACTIVITY

Show the location of the following:

1) Arctic Ocean
2) Arctic Circle
3) Yukon region
4) Yukon River
5) Klondike River
6) Bering Sea
7) Gulf of Alaska

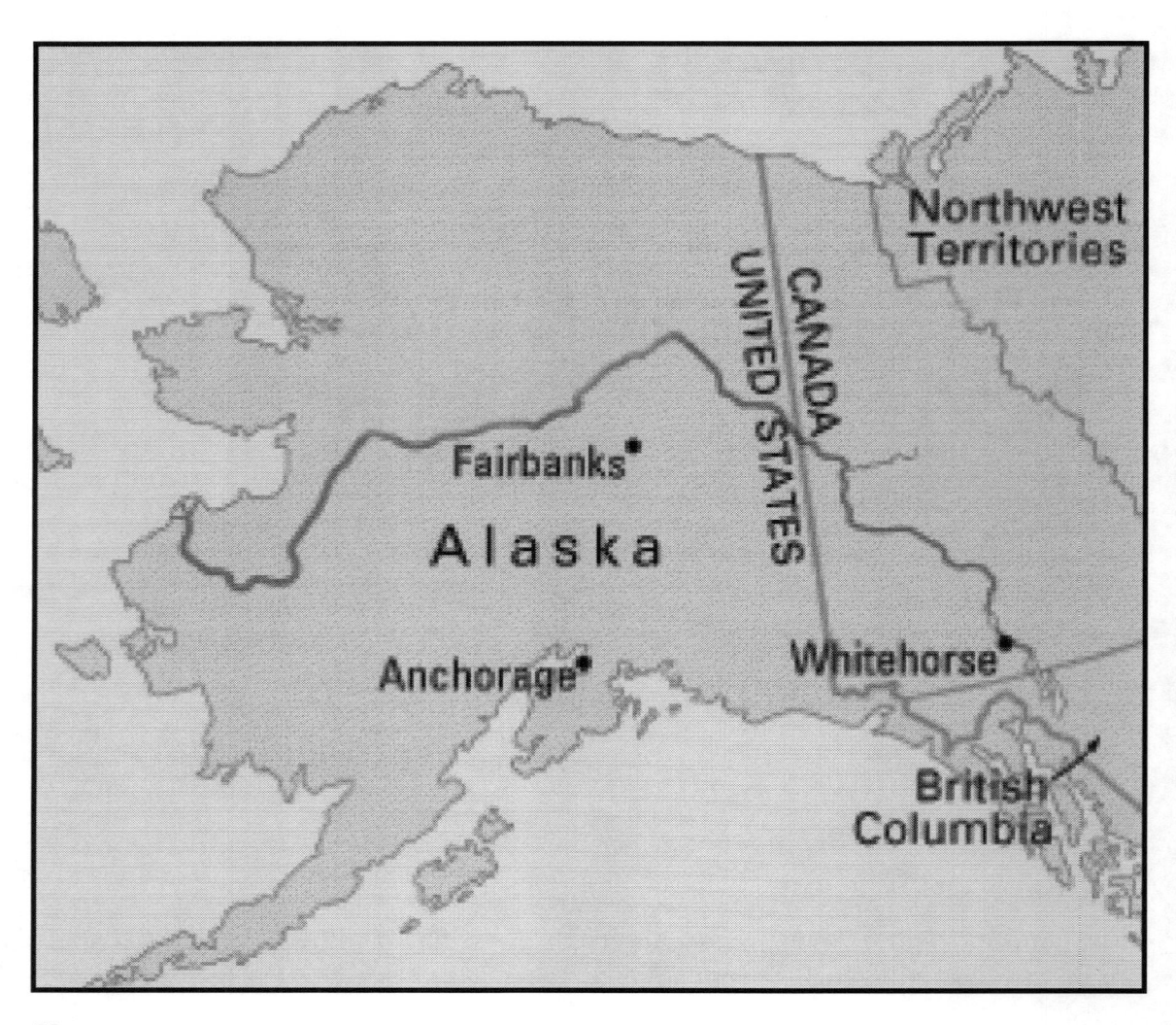

UNIT 3: ALASKA BECOMES U.S. POSSESSION

LESSON 14: ALASKA'S MYSTERIOUS FIRST CENSUS-TAKER

FACTS TO KNOW:

Ivan Petroff – Alaska's first census taker
Territory – An area of land under the authority of a ruler or state
Bidarka – A boat covered in animal skins used by Native people of Alaska

COMPREHENSION QUESTIONS

1) Review Time: In Lesson 12, we learned the definition of a census. Define census.

2) Why was Ivan Petroff chosen to take the Alaska census in 1880? Why was this a controversial choice?

3) How did Ivan Petroff travel to take the census? What obstacles did he encounter?

4) Name some of the people groups that were recorded on the 1880 census.

5) What two important books did Ivan Petroff contribute to?

DISCUSSION QUESTION

(Discuss this question with your teacher or write your answer in essay form below. Use additional paper if necessary.)

What can we learn about Alaska in 1880 from reading what was recorded on the census? Why is this information important?

_____
_____
_____
_____
_____
_____
_____
_____
_____
_____
_____
_____
_____
_____
_____
_____

ENRICHMENT ACTIVITY

Imagine that you are in charge of taking the census for your classroom, family, church group or sports team. Write a list of data about the people in your group. You can track gender, age, ethnicity, occupation, city of residence and any other item that you would like to include in your census.

TO LEARN MORE

Read more about the various people groups of early Alaskan history by visiting http://www.akhistorycourse.org/southcentral-alaska/taming-the-land-of-fire-and-ice

TIME TO REVIEW

Review Chapters 10-14 of your book before moving on to the Unit Review. See how many questions you can answer without looking at your book.

Alaska Purchase
Word Scramble Puzzle
Please unscramble the words below

#	Scrambled	Clue
1.	aribkad	A boat covered in animal skins used by Alaska Natives
2.	rtotrreyi	An area of land under the authority of a ruler or state
3.	secuns	The process of acquiring data about the members of a specific population
4.	relwlagn	Third-oldest community in Alaska
5.	hngirre	A silvery fish that was of great commercial importance as a food fish in Alaska during the 1880s
6.	irhnsaiot	People said Alaska's first census-taker was an able one of these – an expert in past events
7.	scosrcar	Bishop Bompas lived the later years of his life in this settlement
8.	ucsryv	Many early residents in Alaska suffered from this disease caused by a deficiency of vitamin C
9.	stnlratea	Turn one language into another
10.	dilteca	A particular form of a language that is peculiar to a specific region or social group

UNIT 3: ALASKA BECOMES U.S. POSSESSION

REVIEW LESSONS 10-14

Write down what you remember about:

William H. Seward _____

Edouard de Stoecki _____

Sitka _____

Czar Alexander II _____

American Civil War _____

Census _____

Russian Orthodox Church _____

Fort Yukon _____

William Carpenter Bompas _____

Miner _____

George Washington Carmack _____

Ivan Petroff _____

Territory _____

Bidarka _____

Fill in the blanks:

1) U.S. Secretary of State _____ saw the _____ of Alaska long before the United States purchased it in _____.

2) With the _____ War raging during the early _____s, the United States didn't pursue purchase of Alaska until _____ when Seward received word that the _____ were ready to unload the northern property.

3) Many Americans, including legislators, didn't think that the purchase of Alaska was a good idea because _____
_____
_____

4) The amount of the check issued to _____ for the purchase of Alaska was _____. But some people think the check included payment for favors to help the _____ during the American _____.

5) _____ sent the Russian fleet to America in a strategic move during the year _____.

6) Americans eager to engage in _____ and _____ flocked to Alaska before the ink was dry on the ratified treaty to purchase Russia's northern colony.

7) Alaska's _____ _____ industry began in 1878 when 30,000 pounds were caught and preserved with salt in wooden barrels. By the turn of the century, _____ was the leading industry as the _____ industry declined.

8) After arriving in Unalaska in 1824, Father _____ helped spread the _____ doctrine in the Aleutians. He taught Natives in their _____, Aleutian Fox, after creating an _____ and translating textbooks and parts of the Bible.

9) It took _____ more than five years to travel by ship, canoe, on foot and by dog sled from _____ to the _____, where at last he was called to become Bishop of the Yukon.

10) With no roads and only a few Native trails, Alaska's first _____ taker, _____, traveled around some parts of the territory in skin boats called _____. His count totaled 33,426 people, including people from the following groups: _____
_____
_____

Getting an accurate count of people who lived in Alaska after it became part of the United States was challenging. And most Alaska Native people did not know that the Russians had been paid for land that their ancestors had lived on for thousands of years.

People in 1880 Alaska Census
Word Search
Please find the words below

```
R E K R O W Y R E N N A C P
N A I S A C U A C F D R M X
K J B S T T R I I R E N I M
T R T U Q E E S N P N B N Y
D R E N I U H G P U W L N R
H L A D A E A A N L I T N K
A E L P R H R T C I R T V Y
T O N M P T C R T A L A D N
S T A N G E E R D E D T K L
N N W N I O R E E I R T D G
B X Y M L T R N A M T K M Y
R J B E B Y L H L B T M L L
```

Caucasian
Creole
Inuit
Aleut
Tinneh
Tlinget
Haida
Miner

Merchant
Squatter
Trapper
Trader
Fisherman
Cannery worker
Soldier
trapper

65

UNIT 3: ALASKA BECOMES U.S. POSSESSION

UNIT TEST

Choose *two* of the following questions to answer in paragraph form. Use as much detail as possible to completely answer the question. Use extra paper in back of the book if needed.

1) Describe the United States purchase of Alaska. Who saw the value in Alaska and why? How much did America pay for Alaska? When was the transfer finalized?

2) What controversy surrounded the Russian fleet coming to America in 1863? Who sent the fleet? Who was happy to see the fleet arrive in New York and why?

3) Who was the Bishop of the Yukon? How did he start his mission to the Yukon? What did he do for the Native people in this region?

4) What significant information did we learn from the 1880 Alaska census? Who was the census taker? What obstacles did he face while taking the census?

Aunt Phil's Trunk Volume One

UNIT 3: ALASKA BECOMES U.S. POSSESSION

    Review Questions   _____ (possible 12 pts.)
    Fill-the-Blanks   _____ (possible 10 pts.)

Unit Test
  Essay 1
    Demonstrates understanding of the topic   _____ (possible 5 pts.)
    Answered the questions completely and accurately   _____ (possible 5 pts.)
    Composition is neat   _____ (possible 5 pts.)
    Grammar and Spelling   _____ (possible 5 pts.)

  Essay 2
    Demonstrates understanding of the topic   _____ (possible 5 pts.)
    Answered the questions completely and accurately   _____ (possible 5 pts.)
    Composition is neat   _____ (possible 5 pts.)
    Grammar and Spelling   _____ (possible 5 pts.)

        Subtotal Points _____ (possible 62 pts.)

Extra Credit
  Word Puzzle   _____ (5 pt. per completed puzzle)
  Complete an Enrichment Activity   _____ (possible 5 pts.)
  Oral presentation   _____ (possible 10 pts.)

  Total Extra Credit   _____

        Total Unit Points _____

GRADE CHART

A   56-62+ points

B   50-55 points

C   44-49 points

D   37-43 points

UNIT 4: ALASKA'S FIRST GOLD RUSH

LESSON 15: GOLD FOUND IN SOUTHEAST

FACTS TO KNOW:

Prospector – A miner who searches for minerals such as gold, ore and coal
Chief Kowee – The Auk Indian chief who led Joseph Juneau and Richard Harris to gold around Juneau in 1880
Juneau – The first town to be founded in Alaska after it was purchased by the United States
Treadwell Glory Hole – One of the largest quartz lode mines in the world

COMPREHENSION QUESTIONS

1) What major find in Southeast Alaska led thousands of prospectors to the area in 1880? Who made the discovery and in what specific area? _____
_____
_____

2) After this major discovery, Richard Tighe Harris and Joe Juneau established the mining town of _____. How did the dynamics of the area change as a more white prospectors entered the area? _____
_____
_____

3) What purchase did John Treadwell make for $400 from Pierre Joseph "French Pete" Erussard? What amazing discovery did this purchase lead to? _____
_____
_____

4) What company bought out John Treadwell and his investors? When did the purchase occur? What was included in the purchase? _____
_____
_____
_____

DISCUSSION QUESTION

(Discuss this question with your teacher or write your answer in essay form below. Use additional paper if necessary.)

In what ways did the early discovery of gold change Alaska's history? Consider the impact this had on Alaska's population, economy, geography, environment, etc.

ENRICHMENT ACTIVITY

Imagine that you are a journalist covering the discovery of the Treadwell Glory Hole for the local newspaper. Write your story using facts from the chapter and your imagination.

TO LEARN MORE

Read more about the early gold discoveries in Alaska by visiting http://www.akhistory-course.org/americas-territory/gold

Courtesy Alaska State Library

This photograph shows 10 miners working deep inside the Treadwell Ready Bullion mine at the 1,500-foot level in 1908.

The Treadwell operation, which consisted of four mines, was the largest hard rock gold mine in the world, employing more than 2,000 people in Juneau and on Douglas Island in Southeast Alaska. Between 1881 and 1922, more than 3 million troy ounces of gold were extracted (1 troy ounce, which has its origin in the Roman monetary system and is used to weigh precious metals, is about 1.0971 ounces).

The price of gold in 1900 was a stable $20.67 per ounce, which is about $525 in 2017.

UNIT 4: ALASKA'S FIRST GOLD RUSH

LESSON 16: EXPLORING THE NILE OF ALASKA

FACTS TO KNOW:

Lt. Frederick Schwatka – He was commissioned by the U.S. Army to explore the Yukon River

Yukon River – A large river (more than 2,000 miles long) that stretches from Alaska to Canada

Barka – A small-decked boat

COMPREHENSION QUESTIONS

1) Why was Lt. Frederick Schwatka commissioned by the U.S. Army to explore the "Nile of Alaska"? What is the actual name of this river? _____

_____
_____
_____
_____

2) Describe Lt. Schwatca's journey. Who did he travel with? How did he travel?

_____
_____
_____
_____

3) Name three things that Lt. Frederick learned about this region and/or its people.

_____
_____
_____
_____

4) How long did it take Lt. Schwatka to complete his trip? How did his trip end?

_____
_____
_____
_____

DISCUSSION QUESTION

(Discuss this question with your teacher or write your answer in essay form below. Use additional paper if necessary.)

What complaint did Lt. Frederick Schwatka have about the British map after his time on the "Nile of Alaska?"

_____
_____
_____
_____
_____
_____
_____
_____
_____
_____
_____
_____
_____
_____
_____

TO LEARN MORE

To learn more about the Yukon River, look for these books at your local library:
Lifeline to the Yukon – A History of Yukon River Navigation. By Anderson, Barry C. Seattle: Superior Publishing Company, 1983.

Yukon River Steamboats-A Pictorial History. By Cohen, Stan. Missoula, Montana: Pictorial Histories Publishing Company, 1982.

MAP ACTIVITY

Trace the Yukon River on this map. Mark where it begins and ends.

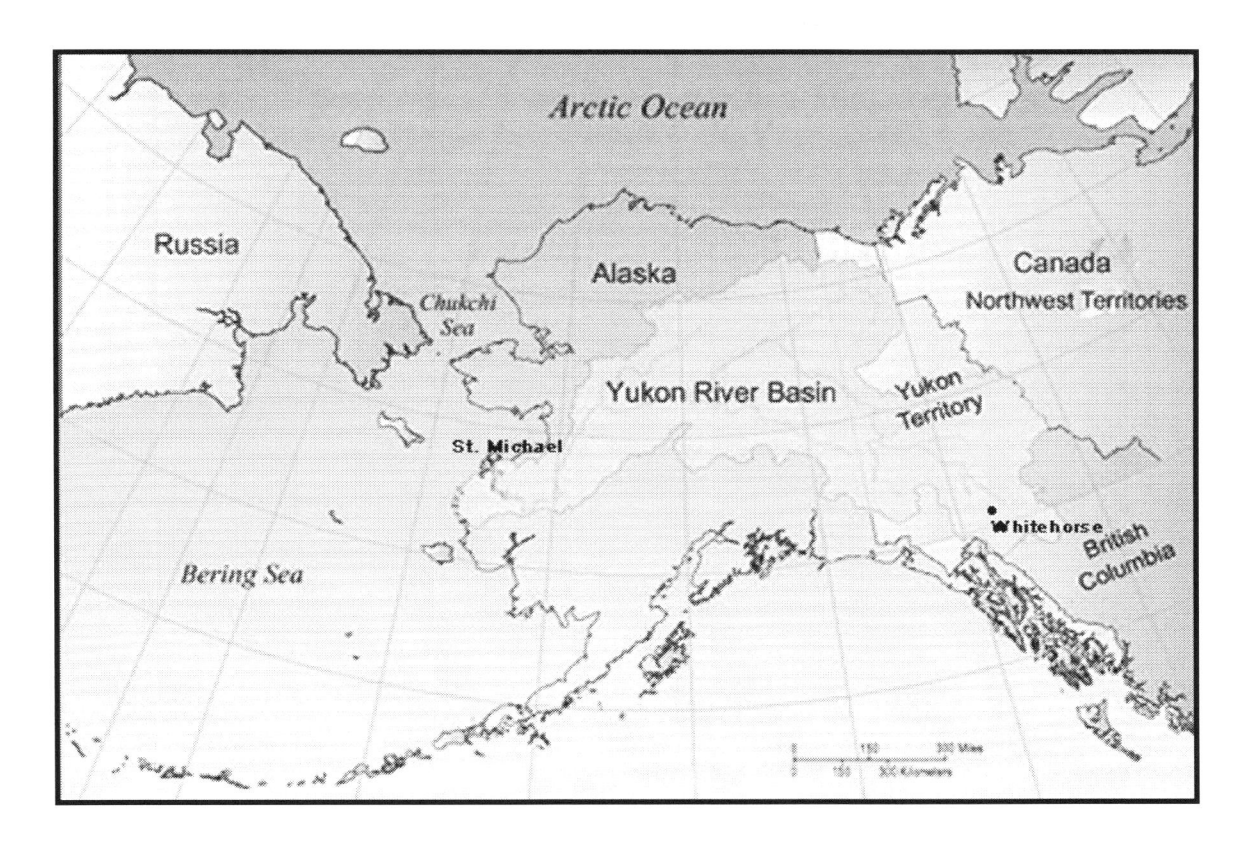

73

First Gold Rush and Exploration
Crossword Puzzle

Read Across and Down clues and fill in blank boxes that match numbers on the clues

Across
4   The highest point of a hill or mountain
7   Closely compacted together, crowded
10 A ship that is propelled by a steam engine
12 Tall, fast-growing trees of north temperate regions
16 A piece of land almost surrounded by water or projecting out into a body of water
18 A hollow or depression in the earth's surface, wholly or partly surrounded by higher land
19 The fixed portion of food or other goods allowed to each person
20 A naturally occurring solid material from which a metal or valuable mineral can be profitably extracted
22 The precious yellow metal that brought many people to Alaska
24 A town named after one of the discoverers of gold in Southeast Alaska in 1880
25 People who search for mineral deposits
30 Longest river in Alaska
31 A length of water wider than a strait, joining two larger areas of water
32 A long, narrow, typically vertical hole that gives access to a mine
33 A sailing ship with two or more masts
35 A place between two mountains where one can go through
36 An important assignment carried out for political, religious or commercial purposes
37 A journey or voyage undertaken by a group of people with a particular purpose
38 Especially fine or decorative clothing
39 Small-decked boat

Down
1   The act of raising or lifting something
2   A small, solid lump of gold
3   Auk chief who took miners Juneau and Harris to Southeast Alaska gold deposit in 1880
5   An island across from Juneau where the Treadwell Mine was established
6   A mineral in the form of a hard, shiny crystal
8   A step like part of a mine where minerals are being extracted
9   The animals of a particular region, habitat or geological period
11 A tributary stream of a river close to or forming part of its source
13 One of the first names for the town of Juneau
14 A river or stream flowing into a larger river or lake
15 A course, way or road for passage or travel
17 A name associated with a group of people rushing to Alaska to search for gold
21 The action of finding something, like Joe Juneau and gold in Silver Bow Basin
22 A narrow and steep-sided ravine marking the course of a fast stream
23 Place where the largest amount of gold, silver, etc., in a particular area can be found
26 Extremely large or great

First Gold Rush and Exploration
Crossword Puzzle

Down (Continued)
27 An amount of material, provisions or money supplied to a prospector to search for ore in return for a share in the resulting profits
28 Travel across or through
29 An alluvial, marine or glacial deposit containing particles of valuable mineral
34 The plants of a particular region, habitat or geological period

UNIT 4: ALASKA'S FIRST GOLD RUSH

LESSON 17: OLD JOHN BREMNER

FACTS TO KNOW:

John Bremner – A Scotsman who came to Alaska to look for gold and was mysteriously killed
Whipsaw – A two-man saw used to cut down trees
John Minook – The man who brought word back to Nukukyet that John Bremner had been killed
Rampart – Once an important trading post and supply center for thousands of miners

COMPREHENSION QUESTIONS

1) What three bodies of water were named after John Bremner? Why? _____
_____
_____

2) What brought John Bremner to the Copper River Valley? Who did he stay with there? Why did he leave? _____
_____
_____

3) How did John Bremner die? Why was there confusion about who killed him? _____
_____
_____
_____

4) What was law enforcement like in that part of Alaska in the 1880s? _____
_____
_____

5) What did the miners do when they heard that John Bremner was killed? How did they settle the dispute in the end? _____
_____
_____

6) What was the name of the first boat to go up the Koyukuk River? _____

DISCUSSION QUESTION

(Discuss this question with your teacher or write your answer in essay form below. Use additional paper if necessary.)

How do you think the case of John Bremner's death might have been different if there was official law enforcement in Koyukuk county at the time of his murder?

_____
_____
_____
_____
_____
_____
_____
_____
_____
_____
_____
_____
_____
_____
_____
_____
_____
_____
_____
_____

ENRICHMENT ACTIVITY

Imagine that you are a prospector in Southeast Alaska in the 1880s. Write a journal entry about one of your adventures. Where did you go? Who did you meet? Were you successful?

TO LEARN MORE

Read more about mining in Alaska by visiting http://www.akhistorycourse.org/americas-territory/alaskas-heritage/chapter-4-15-mining

UNIT 4: ALASKA'S FIRST GOLD RUSH

LESSON 18: RICH NAMES ALONG THE KOYUKUK

FACTS TO KNOW:

Gordon Bettles – Pioneer of the Koyukuk country who set up several "bean shops" (trading posts)

Stampeders – The men and women who rushed to Alaska to search for gold

Revenue Cutter – Steamers that enforced custom and navigation laws under the U.S. Revenue Service, upon which the U.S. Coast Guard later was modeled

COMPREHENSION QUESTIONS

1) What evidence was there that prospectors were looking for gold along the Koyukuk river before the Klondike Gold Rush? _____
_____
_____

2) What are some of the unique features of the Koyukuk as described by Lt. B.H. Camden who traveled there? _____
_____
_____

3) The first streams on the Koyukuk to yield gold in large quantities were _____, _____ and _____ creeks, and as early as 1899, the town of _____ Creek was started.

4) Name three of the places in the Koyukuk region named for prospectors. _____
_____
_____

5) Why did mining in the Koyukuk region become less important after the second boom in 1915? _____
_____
_____

DISCUSSION QUESTIONS

(Discuss this question with your teacher or write your answer in essay form below. Use additional paper if necessary.)

Who was the Blueberry Kid? Summarize his mysterious story.

_____
_____
_____
_____
_____
_____
_____
_____
_____
_____
_____
_____
_____
_____
_____
_____

ENRICHMENT ACTIVITY

Learn more about what life was like for a miner during the gold rush by downloading and reading *The Rush for Gold* comic book. Read it online by visiting http://www.akhistory-course.org/comic/AK_Economy_pp56-109.pdf

TO LEARN MORE

Look for this book at your local library to learn more about the people of the Koyukuk region: *Up the Koyukuk.* Alaska Geographic, 1 0:4 (1983).

TIME TO REVIEW

Review Chapters 15-18 of your book before moving on to the Unit Review. See how many questions you can answer without looking at your book.

Rich Names Along The Koyukuk
Word Search Puzzle
Please find the words below

```
                    K T
                    E Q
                  X O I C
                  J Y R P
                S C C J H D
                  H M R Q L K
              D Y X L H O I Q
                N M S E Y Z B F
              N C L N U T Q E U I
                A I L K A I L K A K
            S I M U L K Q Q P O G Y
              M B K I L I B U N M Q F
            T O O F D L O C U Y A G I H
              P T T S U H U G H E S W K Z
          G A K Y Y E U E D B C T Q C D M
            U W E N J X S O S B N O K U Y Q
          C N G E U K P O V Z O V D Q X P O D
            I Y T R Q Y N G R I A U O Y J S R T
          P I Y I C Q Y Q N H Q L O N I W E O H J
          Y W A I E W S W P C O L L B V W L I I D
          B W I P W T G G J R R Y A A A M Q T R S L E
          G D S Y L A T C W A S P K Y N G T T E J B H
        N H Q E G N L M Q L B U Z A E K R E E T V J V W
        B N P M J G S E I N S T C K C I L X B N H X D O
        T F T S A G M C W M A N L G E W I B M A I A I V G S
        B S S A N Z T A B P S A W E T E K T M L B D F C A Y
                    V U R Q
                    E L V E
                    N E R W
```

Words

Koyukuk	Kakliaklia	Interior
Batzna	Wiseman	Evans Bar
Moses Village	Hughes	Yukon
Allakaket	Bettles	Mastodon Bank
Nok	Coldfoot	Slate Creek

UNIT 4: ALASKA'S FIRST GOLD RUSH

REVIEW LESSONS 15-18

What do you remember about:

Prospectors _____

Chief Kowee _____

Juneau _____

Treadwell Glory Hole _____

Lt. Frederick Schwatka _____

Yukon River _____

Barka _____

John Bremner _____

Whipsaw _____

John Minook _____

Rampart _____

Gordon Bettles _____

Stampeders _____

Revenue Cutter _____

Fill in the blanks:

1) Chief _____ led _____ and _____ to gold near what became the town of _____ in 1880.

2) The influx of white _____ changed the dynamics of the area. _____, _____ and _____ popped up overnight, and by March 1881, monthly _____ service was bringing supplies to the placer miners along Gaustineau Channel.

3) In 1889, the _____ Company bought out _____ and his investors for $4 million. The _____ organization included four mines and the famed _____ Hole.

4) In the summer of 1883, _____ traversed the upper _____ River by raft in order to gather information about _____ _____.

5) _____'s exploration of the _____ River gave the world a firsthand account of the river and the lay of the land. Three things that he learned were: _____
_____
_____

6) _____ lived a life of hardship among the _____ Indians in 1880. He was killed at a _____ camp along the _____ River while putting his boat back in the water.

7) A man named _____, part Russian and part Native, brought news of the murder of _____ to about 60 prospectors. The prospectors decided to avenge his death and _____ the little river steamer named *Explorer* in order to get back to the scene of the crime.

8) Long before the Klondike Gold Rush, evidence of _____ plying the waters of the _____ River were found such as: _____
_____
_____
_____

82

9) Three people, _____, _____ and _____ disappeared from Bettles in _____ after they boarded the _____'s launch.

10) _____ alone reached Nulato and took a steamboat to St. Michael. It is said that he cashed out thousands of dollars of _____ at the Mint, and again in San Francisco.

Old John Bremner

Word Scramble Puzzle

Please unscramble the words below

1. zliezrdg — Having or streaked with gray hair

2. jonualr — A daily record of news and events of a personal nature, similar to a diary

3. pwshwia — A saw with a narrow blade and a handle at both ends, used typically by two people

4. ubrg — Food

5. nveaeg — To punish someone who has harmed you or someone or something that you care about

6. erdmiskba — To leave a ship or boat

7. nreeteiprrt — A person to translates from one language to another

8. neemrbr — Man for whom the John River is named

9. hccae — Food and supplies are kept away from animals in this place

10. inpapotira — A supernatural appearance of a person or thing

UNIT 4: ALASKA'S FIRST GOLD RUSH

UNIT TEST

Choose *two* of the following questions to answer in paragraph form. Use as much detail as possible to completely answer the question. Use extra paper in back of the book if needed.

1) Describe the impact of Alaska's first gold rush. Consider how it changed Alaska's population, economy, geography, etc.

2) Who was commissioned by the U.S. Army to travel the upper Yukon River in 1880? How did he travel up the river? What was the purpose of his trip? What did he learn about the area and its people?

3) Summarize one of the two murder mysteries that happened in the Koyukuk River region. What happened? Who was involved in the story? How did it end?

4) What were some of the features of the Koyukuk River around 1900? What do you know about some of the people of that region?

Aunt Phil's Trunk Volume One

UNIT 4: ALASKA'S FIRST GOLD RUSH

    Review Questions   _____ (possible 14 pts.)
    Fill-the-Blanks   _____ (possible 10 pts.)

Unit Test
  Essay 1
    Demonstrates understanding of the topic   _____ (possible 5 pts.)
    Answered the questions completely and accurately   _____ (possible 5 pts.)
    Composition is neat   _____ (possible 5 pts.)
    Grammar and Spelling   _____ (possible 5 pts.)

  Essay 2
    Demonstrates understanding of the topic   _____ (possible 5 pts.)
    Answered the questions completely and accurately   _____ (possible 5 pts.)
    Composition is neat   _____ (possible 5 pts.)
    Grammar and Spelling   _____ (possible 5 pts.)

                                    Subtotal Points _____ (possible 64 pts.)

Extra Credit
    Word Puzzle   _____ (5 pt. per completed puzzle)
    Complete an Enrichment Activity   _____ (possible 5 pts.)
    Oral presentation   _____ (possible 10 pts.)

    Total Extra Credit   _____

                                    Total Unit Points _____

GRADE CHART

A   58-64+ points

B   51-57 points

C   44-50 points

D   37-43 points

UNIT 5: DREAMS OF GOLD

LESSON 19: ALASKA'S SECOND GOLD RUSH

FACTS TO KNOW:

Peter Doroshin – Mining engineer who explored the Kenai Peninsula in 1849
Grubstake – Usually consisted of enough food and supplies to keep a man for one season
Kenai Peninsula – A large peninsula on the southern coast of Alaska
Hydraulic mining – Use of a high-pressure water jet to break up gravel and make mining more efficient

COMPREHENSION QUESTIONS

1) What was the only recorded official gold-hunting expedition that was made by the Russian-American Company? Who was the prospector? What area did he explore?
_____
_____
_____

2) Why do historians speculate that the Russians did not announce their findings of gold in the Cook Inlet area?
_____
_____
_____

3) Describe Alexander King's prospecting trip to the Kenai Peninsula in 1880. What deal did he arrange with Capt. Charles Swanson? What important discovery did he make? Why was this discovery significant?
_____
_____
_____

4) By the year_____, Alaska's _____ gold rush was in full swing. Articles in large newspapers like the _____ and _____ drew about 3,000 prospectors to the _____.

5) Why was the Cook Inlet gold rush short-lived? How long did it last? How did it end?

6) Why was Alexander King hung on October 2, 1900?

DISCUSSION QUESTION

(Discuss this question with your teacher or write your answer in essay form below. Use additional paper if necessary.)

What have you learned about the mining process? Was it simple or complicated? Explain your answer.

ENRICHMENT ACTIVITY

Imagine that you want to hire a miner to find gold for you in Alaska in 1900. Write a "Help Wanted" classified ad that includes the qualities that you are looking for in a miner and what tools you require the miner to own. Consider what you have learned about successful miners so far in this course.

TO LEARN MORE

Read more about the early mining in Alaska's interior by visiting: http://www.akhistory-course.org/interior-alaska/1869-1896-stars-and-stripes-up-the-river

UNIT 5: DREAMS OF GOLD

LESSON 20: DREAMS OF SALMON TURN TO GOLD

FACTS TO KNOW:

George Washington Carmack – He was credited with starting the Klondike Gold Rush

Tagish Charley (Dawson Charlie) Mason – Codiscoverer of gold at Rabbit Creek that started the Klondike Gold Rush

Skookum Jim Mason – Codiscoverer of gold at Rabbit Creek that started the Klondike Gold Rush

Discovery Claim – The first claim in a region and center point of a mining district

COMPREHENSION QUESTIONS

1) Unlike most hard-working prospectors, George Washington Carmack had time for the finer things in life. What kind of "finer things" did he enjoy?

2) George Washington Carmack had a premonition while sitting in the ruins of old Fort Selkirk in 1896. What was his premonition? What did he do after he had the premonition? How did that premonition lead him to the Throndiuk (later called Klondike)?

3) Why is August 17, 1896, a memorable day that is still celebrated in Yukon Territory? What happened on this day?

4) Explain the dispute between George Washington Carmack, Tagish Charley and Skookum Jim about the discovery claim. What did they eventually agree upon and why?

5) What did George Washington Carmack do on the way to the mining recorder's office that sent a rush of prospectors to the Klondike?

6) Why did George Washington Carmack eventually leave his wife, Kate, and end his partnerships with Tagish Charley and Skookum Jim?

7) How did the discovery of gold in the Klondike in 1896 help the United States out of a deep depression?

DISCUSSION QUESTION

(Discuss this question with your teacher or write your answer in essay form below. Use additional paper if necessary.)

In what ways do you think the Klondike gold rush changed Alaska's economy and population?

ENRICHMENT ACTIVITY

Chapter 20 began with a poem written by George Washington Carmack. Find another poem written by a famous person in Alaska's history. See if you can discover what happened in the poet's life to cause him or her to write that particular poem. Use books and online resources to do your research.

TO LEARN MORE

Read about what happened to the *S.S. Portland* by visiting http://www.akhistorycourse.org/americas-territory/wreck-of-the-ss-portland-found

Prospecting in the Klondike was tough work.

UNIT 5: DREAMS OF GOLD

LESSON 21: LUCKIEST MAN ON THE KLONDIKE

FACTS TO KNOW:

Clarence Berry – "The luckiest man on the Klondike" who strikes it rich after hearing of George Washington Carmack's discovery

Throndiuk – Indian word for Klondike

Bonanza Creek – Rabbit Creek was later renamed Bonanza Creek after gold was discovered there

S.S. Portland – One of two steamships filled with gold and miners from the Klondike

S.S. Excelsior – One of two steamships filled with gold and miners from the Klondike

COMPREHENSION QUESTIONS

1) How did Clarence Berry begin his prospecting journey? What obstacles did he face?

2) Who was the "Bride of the Klondike"? What advice did she give to other women travelers to Alaska?

3) How did George Washington Carmack's announcement at Bill McPhee's Bar change Clarence Berry's fortune?

4) Describe the process that Clarence Berry and his partner, Anton Stander, used to mine in the winter.

5) How did the Berrys travel back to California? What did they bring back with them? What did they tell reporters about the Klondike?

_____
_____
_____

6) How did Clarence Berry repay Bill McPhee? What did he repay him for?

_____
_____
_____

DISCUSSION QUESTION

(Discuss this question with your teacher or write your answer in essay form below. Use additional paper if necessary.)

What was the difference between how Clarence Berry and George Washington Carmack handled their new-found wealth?

_____
_____
_____
_____
_____
_____
_____
_____
_____
_____
_____
_____

TO LEARN MORE

To read more about the Klondike Gold Rush, look for this book at your local library: *One Man's Gold Rush: A Klondike Album*. Seattle: University of Washington Press and Vancouver: Douglas and McIntyre, 1967.

TIME TO REVIEW

Review Chapters 19-21 of your book before moving on to the Unit Review. See how many questions you can answer without looking at your book.

UNIT 5: DREAMS OF GOLD

REVIEW LESSONS 19-21

What do you remember about:

Peter Doroshin _____

Grubstake _____

Kenai Peninsula _____

Hydraulic mining _____

George Washington Carmack _____

Tagish Charley (Dawson Charlie) Mason _____

Skookum Jim Mason _____

Discovery Claim _____

Clarence Berry _____

Throndiuk _____

Bonanza Creek _____

S.S. Portland _____

S.S. Excelsior _____

Fill in the blanks:

1) In the year _____, the Russian-American Company sent mining engineer _____ to the _____ area to search for gold.

2) Around 1888, a prospector named _____ arrived at _____ and convinced Capt. Charles Swanson, who owned a trading post, to _____ him for two summers and a winter.

3) Mining was _____. The liberal use of a _____ and a _____, as well as a _____, was all that most men needed.

4) While waiting for his friends _____ and _____ to join him, Skookum Jim looked at the sand of the creek where he'd gone to get a drink. He found _____, he said, in greater quantities than he had ever seen before. That was on the date _____, a memorable day that still is celebrated in the _____ Territory.

5) _____ thought the _____ on Rabbit Creek should be his by right of discovery, but Carmack told him that an Indian would not be allowed to record it.

6) After _____, _____ and _____ discovered _____ along Rabbit Creek, they renamed their find "_____" and built sluice boxes to sift out the _____.

7) In 1896, the United States was in the third year of a severe _____. The Klondike gold loosened up _____ all over the world, stimulated inventiveness and gave _____ to many. It was the last of the great international _____.

8) A few years before Lady Luck showered riches on _____, the "luckiest man on the _____" didn't have enough money to pay his room rent or ask his sweetheart _____ to marry him.

94

9) To make ends meet, _____ took a job tending bar at _____. He was bartending the day that _____ came rushing in to tell of striking it rich on the _____.

10) When the S.S. _____ docked in _____ on July 14, 1897, the _____ told reporters, "_____ is the richest gold field in the world."

11) _____ and _____ carried _____ off the steamship.

95

UNIT 5: DREAMS OF GOLD

UNIT TEST

Choose *two* of the following questions to answer in paragraph form. Use as much detail as possible to completely answer the question. Use extra paper in back of the book if needed.

1) How did the Cook Inlet gold rush begin? Who made the first discovery and when? How did it end and why?

2) Compare and contrast the stories of George Washington Carmack and Clarence Berry. What similarities can you find about their journeys to the Klondike? What was different? Compare how Carmack and Berry handled their new-found wealth.

3) What did you learn about the mining process of the 1800s? What kind of tools were used? How did the process change during the winter?

4) How did the Klondike gold rush impact the United States economy in 1896? How did it impact the history of Alaska?

Aunt Phil's Trunk Volume One

UNIT 5: DREAMS OF GOLD

    Review Questions   _____ (possible 13 pts.)
    Fill-the-Blanks   _____ (possible 11 pts.)

Unit Test
  Essay 1
    Demonstrates understanding of the topic   _____ (possible 5 pts.)
    Answered the questions completely and accurately   _____ (possible 5 pts.)
    Composition is neat   _____ (possible 5 pts.)
    Grammar and Spelling   _____ (possible 5 pts.)

  Essay 2
    Demonstrates understanding of the topic   _____ (possible 5 pts.)
    Answered the questions completely and accurately   _____ (possible 5 pts.)
    Composition is neat   _____ (possible 5 pts.)
    Grammar and Spelling   _____ (possible 5 pts.)

                                    Subtotal Points _____ **(possible 64 pts.)**

Extra Credit
  Word Puzzle   _____ (5 pt. per completed puzzle)
  Complete an Enrichment Activity   _____ (possible 5 pts.)
  Oral presentation   _____ (possible 10 pts.)

  Total Extra Credit   _____

                                    Total Unit Points _____

GRADE CHART

A   57-64+ points

B   50-56 points

C   43-49 points

D   36-42 points

Dreams of Gold
Crossword Puzzle

Read Across and Down clues and fill in blank boxes that match numbers on the clues

Across
2 The name of the creek where George Washington Carmack and his friends found gold
6 This mining town bordered Resurrection Creek
7 This mining town grew to be the largest settlement in Cook Inlet after gold was discovered in 1896
9 A tool for breaking hard rock, with a long wooden handle and a curved metal bar
11 This ship arrived in Seattle on July 17, 1897, loaded with gold from the Klondike
16 A boat with a narrow, flat bottom, high bow and flaring sides
17 One of George Washington Carmack's friends
18 A bag miners used to carry gold
22 A person who searches for gold
23 Waste left over after gold has been processed
26 Alexander King rowed up this Arm, known for its swift tides, in 1888
27 Unchartered territory
28 George Washington Carmack had a premonition while sitting among the rocks at this location
29 This ship carried Klondike gold to San Francisco in July 1897
30 A place of excavating, especially for gold
31 One of George Washington Carmack's friends
32 A risky or daring journey or undertaking
33 A strong feeling that something is about to happen

Down
1 A long arduous journey, typically on foot
3 Rabbit Creek was renamed this after Carmack discovered gold there in 1896
4 A person newly arrived in the mining districts of Alaska
5 A small shelter made of wood and situated in a wild or remote area
8 A large flat-bottomed boat with broad square ends used to haul gold
10 Caribou Crossing was later renamed this name
11 Supplies
12 A form of mining that extracts gold from a placer deposit using a pan
13 A small piece of land near Clarence Berry's claim that was rich with gold
14 George Washington Carmack told the people at this settlement about his gold discovery
15 To wash gold by rinsing with water
19 Area of the Yukon where George Washington Carmack found a fortune in gold
20 Creek where gold was found in Cook Inlet area in 1896
21 The hard area of rock in the ground that holds up the loose soil above

Dreams of Gold
Crossword Puzzle

Down (Continued)
24 Port where the *Excelsior* and the *Portland* loaded up with gold and gold miners to head to Seattle and San Francisco in 1897
25 A tract of land having access to a vein or lode of gold

UNIT 6: RUSH TO THE KLONDIKE

LESSON 22: DAWSON IS BORN

FACTS TO KNOW:

Dawson City – A city on the Yukon that became the center of the Klondike Gold Rush
Joseph Ladue – Founder of Dawson City
Kate Ryan – Canadian nurse who traveled to Dawson City for adventure

COMPREHENSION QUESTIONS

1) Who was Dawson City named for? Why? _____
_____
_____

2) What offer did Joseph Ladue make to Lt. Frederick Schwatka? What happened next?
_____
_____
_____
_____

3) How did Joseph Ladue profit off the gold rush? How did the growing population increase his business? _____
_____
_____
_____

4) Dawson City became the largest city north of San Francisco and west of Winnipeg. What were some of the amenities that Dawson City offered? _____
_____
_____
_____

5) Why were fires a common occurrence in Dawson City? What was the fire department like? _____
_____
_____

DISCUSSION QUESTION

(Discuss this question with your teacher or write your answer in essay form below. Use additional paper if necessary.)

Who was Kate Ryan? Why did she come to the Klondike? What did she do when she got there?

ENRICHMENT ACTIVITY

The gold rush provided an opportunity for people like Joseph Ladue to establish a new city. Create your own 1896 gold rush city. Draw a map of your city and label all of the important landmarks in your city. Consider what businesses, services and organizations would be important for the people of your city.

TO LEARN MORE

Look for this book at your local library:
The Klondike Fever, Pierre Berton. New York: Alfred Knopf, 1967.

UNIT 6: RUSH TO THE KLONDIKE

LESSON 23: ST. MICHAEL AWAKENS

FACTS TO KNOW:

St. Michael – Once a sleepy old Russian village, it became a hub for those coming from and going to the Yukon

Steamer – A little boat typically designed to transport a small number of people, but were often overcrowded to carry stampeders to and from St. Michael

All-water route – Route people took to the Klondike gold fields by steamship from Seattle to St. Michael and then on smaller boats on the Yukon River to Dawson

COMPREHENSION QUESTIONS

1) How did St. Michael "awaken" on June 25, 1897? _____
_____
_____
_____

2) Explain why St. Michael was an important stop to the Yukon? How did this fact create a need in St. Michael? _____
_____
_____
_____
_____

3) Why did the U.S. War department build Fort St. Michael? _____
_____
_____
_____

4) What were the conditions like on the little steamers coming out of St. Michael? How long was the trip along the Yukon River from St. Michael to Dawson?
_____
_____
_____

5) What were the alternate land routes to the Yukon? Why would some prospectors prefer one of the land routes? _____

DISCUSSION QUESTION

(Discuss this question with your teacher or write your answer in essay form below. Use additional paper if necessary.)

It was a long, hard, expensive journey to get to the Klondike. If you lived during the Klondike Gold Rush period, would you consider making the trip? Why or why not?

TO LEARN MORE

Look for this book at your local library: *Sternwheels on the Yukon,* Arthur Knutson. Snohomish, Washington: Snohomish Publishing Company, 1979

Read more about river transportation in Alaska by visiting http://www.akhistorycourse.org/americas-territory/rivers-get-people-and-freight-inland

MAP ACTIVITY – Locate the following places on the map below using Page 209 of your textbook as a reference:

1) Skagway
2) Deya
3) Chilkoot Trail
4) Sheep Camp
5) The Scales
6) White Pass Trail
7) Bennett
8) Chilkoot Pass

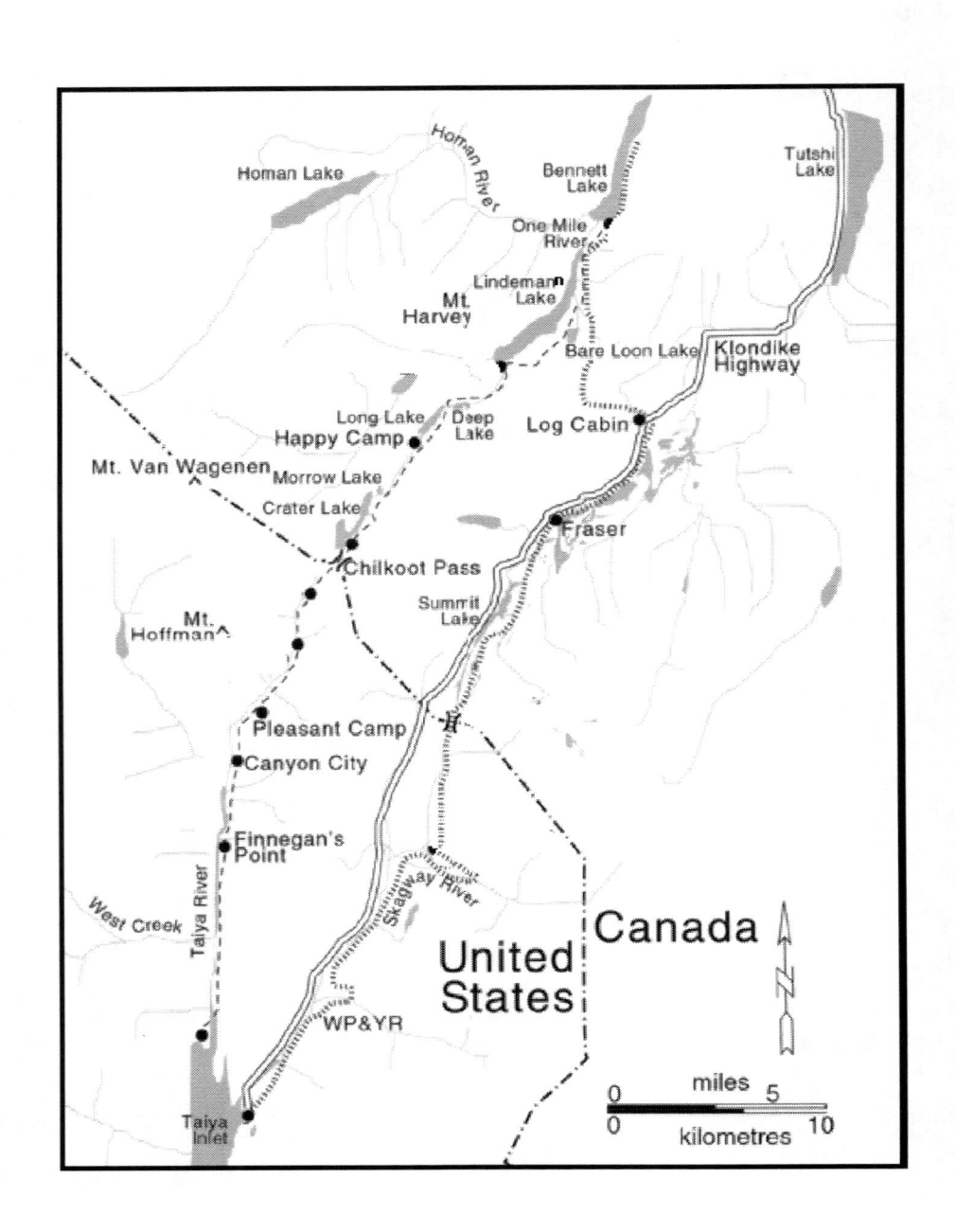

RUSH TO THE KLONDIKE
WORD SEARCH PUZZLE
Find the words in the list below

```
A E W R A N G E L L I T           S V U T Z F
B         K Y D M M B V             T E P L
K         X A V K D K L C           Z X
N         V N O S W A D S     W S   B Y
Q         G V Y A B Q T S     U J   D A
U N M E K I D N O L K K A D C B P S K H T P L T
G N V B K I G C X S R F P X O J N I L E A D D D M J
K A C M R M P E S R O H E T I H W Z B P T E D Q X V
N M W Q W R F K V C G H T N P R V S T M I C H A E L
W E W V I O P I Y L S W I P I T A R O N E L G G D F
H D Y T I C E L C R I H C P K I U T T E N N E B
N N W L W Q O D X A Z C W U Z U I V N M R J A Q Y
L I W C H I L K O O T P A S S C K T X I L W L M D
U L O D H Y C K Y Z F G C J P L U V S Q K R P M L Y
I E L I M Y T R O F I P Z Y F S H E E P C A M P B H E
B Z K Y A W G A K S N C G N S K C A N A D A P K B I W A
T W H F M Z F A T L I N R D R N H H I J M U T H V Q S P P
        B I O B M   H Y T O K   Q B J P L   X Z X B Y
        N I G       J L G       S C L       R U Q
```

DAWSON	KLONDIKE	CHILKOOT PASS
FORTYMILE	STIKINE	GLENORA
ATLIN	WHITEHORSE	ST MICHAEL
SKAGWAY	DYEA	BENNETT
CIRCLE CITY	WRANGELL	CANADA
SHEEP CAMP	LINDEMANN	WHITE PASS

105

UNIT 6: RUSH TO THE KLONDIKE

LESSON 24: TRAILS TO GOLD

FACTS TO KNOW:

White Pass Trail – A land trail route to the Yukon, starting at Skagway, that was used at the beginning of the Klondike Gold Rush

Chilkoot Pass Trail – A 33-mile steep trail to the Yukon starting just north of Skagway

Outfit – The load of supplies that a stampeder carried with them on a prospecting trip

Mounties – Members of the North-West Mounted Police, forerunner of Royal Canadian Mounted Police

COMPREHENSION QUESTIONS

1) What was "Dead Horse Trail"? How did it get that nickname? Why was it closed in September 1897? _____
_____
_____

2) Name some of the supplies needed for a trip to the Klondike. How much did the typical load of supplies for one miner weigh? _____
_____
_____

3) What are some of the ways that the stampeders got their supplies to the Klondike?
_____
_____
_____

4) What did Mike Mahoney carry up the Chilkoot Trail in an attempt to get it to the Klondike and why? Why was he turned away? _____
_____
_____
_____

5) Almost none of the _____ gold seekers who left for the _____ in the fall of 1897 by way of the _____ trail, _____ trail, the _____ trail or the all-water route made it to _____ by the winter. Once they reached _____ in 1898, most stampeders found the cost of living _____ and the good gold claims already taken.

DISCUSSION QUESTION

(Discuss this question with your teacher or write your answer in essay form below. Use additional paper if necessary.)

Summarize the options that prospectors had to travel from Seattle to the Yukon. What were the options for all-water routes? What were the options for land routes?

_____
_____
_____
_____
_____
_____
_____
_____
_____
_____
_____
_____
_____
_____
_____

ENRICHMENT ACTIVITY

Imagine that you are a stampeder traveling to the Klondike in 1897. Write a letter to a family member about your adventures. Use what you have learned about the various route options that stampeders had to choose from. Which route did you take? How are the conditions? Who did you meet? What did you see?

TO LEARN MORE

To read more about the Klondike Gold Rush, look for this book at your local library: *One Man's Gold Rush: A Klondike Album.* Seattle: University of Washington Press and Vancouver: Douglas and McIntyre, 1967.

UNIT 6: RUSH TO THE KLONDIKE

LESSON 25: GOLD RUSH TRAILS PHOTO ESSAY

Fill in the blanks:

1) Stampeders traveling from Skagway climbed either the _____ or _____ trails; and those who took steamers all the way to _____ transferred to small boats to chug up the _____ River to _____ City.

2) Stampeders loaded up pack horses and hauled their _____-pound outfits up the trails. The _____ appeared a less arduous route over the mountains than the steep _____, but it had a series of narrow climbs on a rocky switchback path. This route became known as "_____," because 3,000 pack animals died along the trail in less than three months.

3) The majority of stampeders heading to the Klondike chose the _____ trail. After disembarking at the Southeast Alaska town of _____, they hiked five miles to Dyea, where they then had the 3,739-foot _____ summit to reach.

4) Shortly after the initial rush, enterprising stampeders rigged an aerial _____ to haul prospectors' _____ up to the summit of the _____ for a fee. Most prospectors didn't have any money to spare, however, and hauled their own _____ up the trail or hired _____ for between 12 cents and $1 a load.

5) _____ trips were necessary to haul supplies up the _____, as a strong man could not carry more than _____ pounds on his back at a time. Stampeders carried _____ that were comprised of items such as: _____
_____

6) Klondikers had to pass inspection with _____ who inspected each _____ to make sure that everyone who crossed over into Canada had the required _____.

108

7) Prospectors who finally made it to _____ City – by way of the all-water, the _____, _____ or _____ routes – found the settlement blossoming in the wilderness. However, they also found the _____ high and most of the _____ claimed, so many _____.

8) Three lucky prospectors, _____, _____ and _____ discovered gold at _____ on _____. Most prospectors found _____. But the prospect of sudden riches was not all that mattered. For many who made the incredible journey, the Klondike represented _____.

ENRICHMENT ACTIVITY

Write your own photo essay using one or two pictures from Chapter 25. Create your own story about what happened in the picture. Write at least one paragraph, and include as many details as possible.

TO LEARN MORE

Klondike Letters: The Correspondence of a Gold Seeker in 1898. Anchorage: Alaska Northwest Publishing Company, 1984. Book insert in The Alaska Journal (4) (Autumn 1984).

UNIT 6: RUSH TO THE KLONDIKE

LESSON 26: JACK DALTON BUILDS TOLL ROAD

FACTS TO KNOW:

Jack Dalton – A frontiersman who opened the Dalton Trail toll road
E.J. Glave – Jack Dalton's companion who helped him explore the toll road route
Dalton Trail – A toll road from Pyramid Harbor on the Lynn Canal in Southeastern Alaska to the Yukon
Toll road – A road that travelers must pay to use

COMPREHENSION QUESTIONS

1) Who was the Dalton Trail named after? When did it open? _____
_____
_____

2) What part of the current Alaska road system in Southeast Alaska did part of this toll road eventually become? _____

3) Jack Dalton left his life on the sea and joined the expedition of _____
_____ in _____ to explore Mount _____
_____.

4) Describe Jack Dalton. Why was he so well suited to run a toll road? _____
_____
_____
_____

5 What purpose did the toll road serve during the gold rush? _____
_____
_____

6) Why was it important that Jack Dalton was able to interact with the Native people? Why did the Natives in the area try to discourage Dalton from opening the toll road?
_____
_____
_____

DISCUSSION QUESTION

(Discuss this question with your teacher or write your answer in essay form below. Use additional paper if necessary.)

The growing population in Alaska provided many new economic opportunities to open businesses, found new cities or open a toll road like Jack Dalton. Name three examples of these economic opportunities from Unit 6.

TO LEARN MORE

Read more about the Dalton Trail and other overland routes in Alaska by visiting: http://www.akhistorycourse.org/americas-territory/overland-routes-develop

TIME TO REVIEW

Review Chapters 22-26 of your book before moving on to the Unit Review. See how many questions you can answer without looking at your book.

UNIT 6: RUSH TO THE KLONDIKE

REVIEW LESSONS 22-26

What do you remember about:

Dawson City _____

Joseph Ladue _____

Kate Ryan _____

St. Michael _____

Passenger Steamer _____

All-water route _____

White Pass Trail _____

Chilkoot Pass Trail _____

Outfit _____

Mounties _____

Jack Dalton _____

E.J. Glave _____

Dalton Trail _____

Toll road _____

Fill in the blanks:

1) On _____, _____founded _____City, named after _____, head of the Geological Survey of Canada, who had surveyed the area and noted its possibilities for _____ a decade before.

2) It's estimated that _____ people set out on the rugged journey north, and that between _____ and _____ actually reached the Klondike area.

3) Dawson became the _____ north of San Francisco and west of Winnipeg and boasted nearly 40,000 residents at its height, providing those citizens with _____
_____.

4) In no time at all, Dawson resembled a large cosmopolitan city with _____ _____.

5) On June 25, 1897, the sleepy old Russian town of _____ awoke when the river steamer named *Alice* arrived with 25 miners from _____ carrying $500,000 among them in gold dust.

6) Many of the stampeders heading to the Klondike decided to travel by an all-_____ route. They took large steamships from Seattle to _____, but then had to find alternative means to travel the _____ River to _____. All passengers and cargo had to land at _____ and transfer to small steamers.

7) Many adventures who chose not to travel the water route through _____ tackled their choice of two other _____ routes instead: the _____ Pass and the _____ Pass trails.

8) The _____ Pass was a less arduous trail over the mountains than the steep _____. It started at _____, and the first several miles of _____ Pass had good road with a gentle upward grade wide enough for _____. However, it eventually earned the name "_____," because 3,000 _____ died along the route in less than three months.

113

9) The 33-mile _____ pass trail, which started one mile from _____, just north of _____, also had steep, forbidding grades, but it turned out to be the most direct route to lakes _____ and _____, the headwaters of the _____.

10) Each man would need enough food, clothing and working materials to last at least _____. Other essentials for a gold-seeker's outfit included: _____
_____
_____.

11) _____, a feisty man who arrived in Alaska in the 1880s, became a member of _____ exploration party and established a _____ to the Yukon gold fields based on his travels.

12) Parts of that Southeast Alaska toll road can be traveled today along the _____
_____.

Rush to the Klondike
Word Scramble
Please unscramble the words below

1. foCfee — A drink made from roasted and ground beanlike seeds, usually served hot

2. aoBnc — Thin strips of cured meat from the sides and belly of a pig

3. ruoFl — A powder obtained by grinding grain, typically wheat, and used to make bread

4. Rcei — Small white or brown grains that come from Asian plant and used for food

5. seaBn — An edible seed, typically kidney-shaped, growing in long pods on certain leguminous plants

6. hacMets — A short slender piece of material tipped with a mixture that produces fire when scratched

7. lsiUsent — Forks, spoons and knives, for instance

8. hltoCnig — Things that people wear

9. Blenatk — A covering used especially on a bed to keep you warm

10. Seohvl — A tool with a broad flat blade used for moving dirt

UNIT 6: RUSH TO THE KLONDIKE

UNIT TEST

Choose *three* of the following questions to answer in paragraph form. Use as much detail as possible to completely answer the question. Use extra paper in back of the book if needed.

1) When was Dawson City founded and by whom? Describe how the gold rush impacted Dawson's growth? What luxuries did the city offer?

2) How did St. Michael become a hub for Klondikers? What industries were important in St. Michael because of the gold rush?

3) Describe the all-water routes to the Klondike. Give details of each step that the prospectors needed to take to get to the Klondike. How long did this trip usually take? What were the conditions like?

4) Describe the two major land routes to the Klondike. Give details of each step that the prospectors needed to take to get to the Klondike. What were the conditions like?

5) What was the typical outfit like of a stampeder traveling to the Klondike? How much did it weigh? What was usually included in the outfit?

_____
_____
_____
_____
_____
_____
_____
_____
_____
_____
_____
_____
_____
_____
_____

Aunt Phil's Trunk Volume One

UNIT 6: RUSH TO THE KLONDIKE

    Review Questions   _____ (possible 14 pts.)
    Fill-the-Blanks   _____ (possible 12 pts.)

Unit Test
  Essay 1
    Demonstrates understanding of the topic   _____ (possible 5 pts.)
    Answered the questions completely and accurately   _____ (possible 5 pts.)
    Composition is neat   _____ (possible 5 pts.)
    Grammar and Spelling   _____ (possible 5 pts.)

  Essay 2
    Demonstrates understanding of the topic   _____ (possible 5 pts.)
    Answered the questions completely and accurately   _____ (possible 5 pts.)
    Composition is neat   _____ (possible 5 pts.)
    Grammar and Spelling   _____ (possible 5 pts.)

  Essay 3
    Demonstrates understanding of the topic   _____ (possible 5 pts.)
    Answered the questions completely and accurately   _____ (possible 5 pts.)
    Composition is neat   _____ (possible 5 pts.)
    Grammar and Spelling   _____ (possible 5 pts.)

                    Subtotal Points _____ (possible 86 pts.)

Extra Credit
    Word Puzzle   _____ (5 pt. per completed puzzle)
    Complete an Enrichment Activity   _____ (possible 5 pts.)
    Oral presentation   _____ (possible 10 pts.)

    Total Extra Credit   _____

                    Total Unit Points _____

GRADE CHART

A   80-86+ points

B   69-79 points

C   62-68 points

D   54-61 points

Rush to the Klondike
Crossword Puzzle

Read Across and Down clues and fill in blank boxes that match numbers on the clues

Across
1. The top of the Chilkoot Trail is one of these
2. A crude railroad of wooden rails or of wooden rails capped with metal treads
4. Most miners had this – a short coat or jacket made of a thick, heavy woolen cloth, typically with a plaid design
5. The man who founded Dawson
10. Mike Mahoney carried this up the Chilkoot Pass Trail for a troupe of female entertainers
12. Canadian policemen
14. A business that cuts logs into lumber
15. Sleeping quarters on a ship
16. An acquired or natural skill at performing a task
18. Those who were among the first to explore or settle Alaska
20. The buildup of this flammable oily substance caused many fires in gold-rush towns
22. Clothes made from deer hide
24. This man established the only successful toll road into the Klondike area
26. The long tube that takes smoke and gases from a stove up through a roof
30. Woman who came north and became first female constable for North West Mounted Police
31. The title of newspaper stories that is printed in large letters at the top
32. Fire engines that were used from 1860 to 1920
33. Providing an easy and quick way to solve a problem or do something
34. A town like Dawson that grows rapidly as a result of sudden prosperity
35. These pack animals used to carry supplies along gold rush trails

Down
1. A sudden rush of people to the Klondike
3. Involving or requiring strenuous effort; difficult and tiring
6. A high, soft boot worn in the Arctic that is traditionally made from sealskin
7. The *SS Portland* and *SS Excelsior* are both this type of boat
8. More than 1,000 of these were carved into the Chilkoot Pass
9. The men who were paid to carry supplies up the Chilkoot Trail
11. A member of an Indian people of southeastern Alaska belonging to Tlingit group of Indians
13. A person or animal with whom one spends a lot of time or with whom one travels
17. A type of entertainment including short acts, such as comedy, singing and dancing
19. A person, especially a man, who lives in sparsely settled regions
21. A road, trail or section of railroad tracks that has many sharp turns for climbing a steep hill
23. The area at the base of the Chilkoot Trail was called this name
25. A person who searches for gold

Rush to the Klondike
Crossword Puzzle

Down (Continued)
27 A natural environment on earth where human activity has not yet reached
28 A large building that offered entertainment to gold rush m1ners
29 A type of handsaw worked by two people
34 A covering of leather, rubber or the like for the foot and lower part of the leg

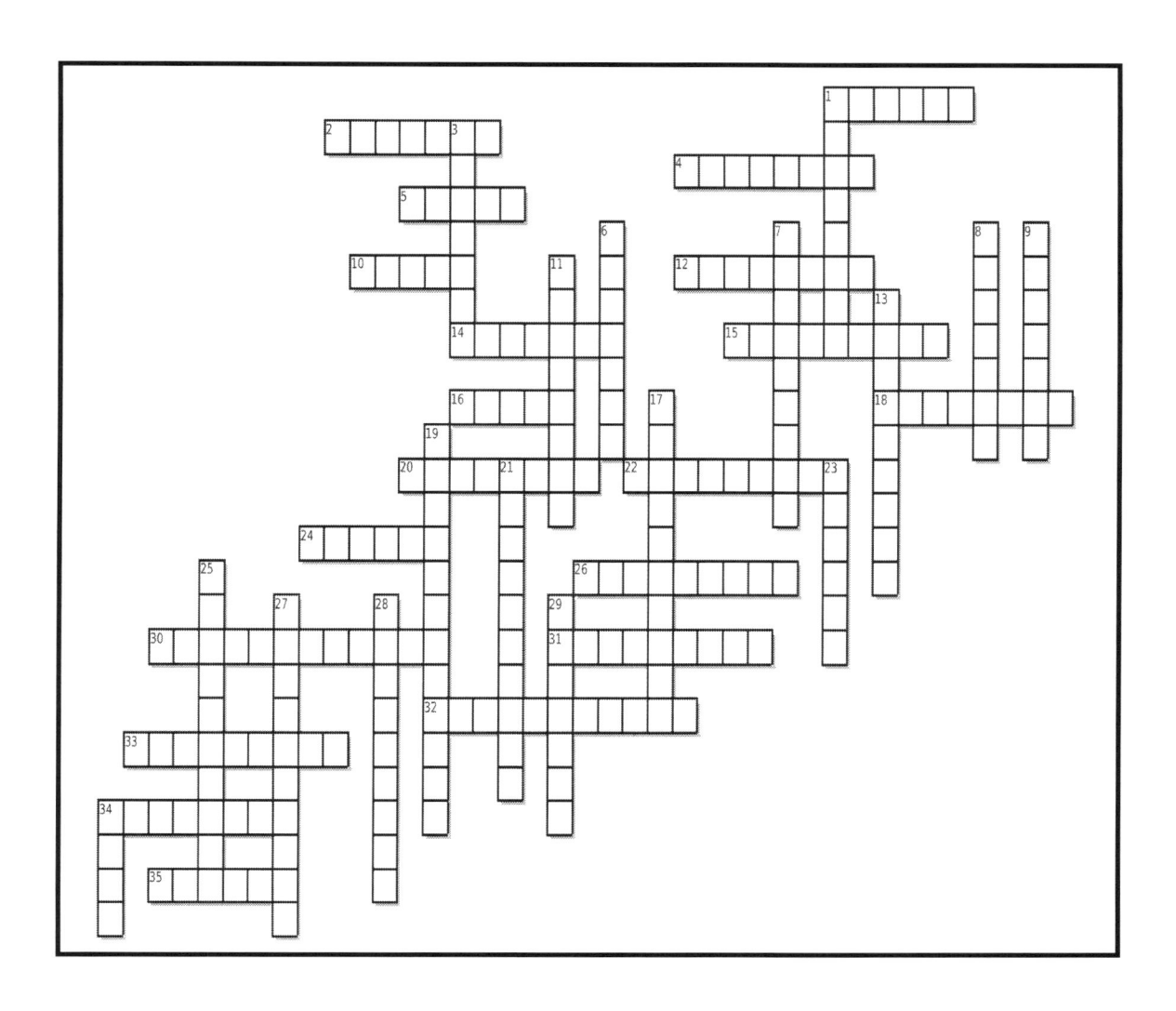

Stampeders could socialize along the Chilkoot Pass Trail, as the photo above taken in 1898 at Sheep Camp shows. The Mascott "hotel" offered hot drinks, meals, lunches and beds. But once the prospectors reached the Klondike gold fields, life could be solitary, as the photo on the bottom shows.

UNIT 7: SEA CAPTAINS, SCOUNDRELS AND NUNS

LESSON 27: SEA CAPTAIN STIFLES MUTINY

FACTS TO KNOW:

Captain Johnny O'Brien – The Irish sea captain of the *Utopia*
Utopia – Captain Johnny O'Brien's steamship
Shanghaied – A term for kidnapping a man and forcing him to work at sea for no pay
Mutiny – Openly refusing to obey someone in authority

COMPREHENSION QUESTIONS

1) What country was Captain Johnny O'Brien from? How did he come to work at sea at the age of 16?

2) Where did the term "shanghaied" come from? How did the California gold rush of 1848 cause a need for more sailors?

3) What happened when Captain Johnny O'Brien became very ill on the *Utopia*?

4) Who nursed the captain back to health?

5) Describe the mutiny that almost occurred on the *Utopia*. Who helped Captain O'Brien?

DISCUSSION QUESTION

(Discuss this question with your teacher or write your answer in essay form below. Use additional paper if necessary.)

In this lesson, we learned that men were drugged, kidnapped and forced to work on ships for no pay. What do you think about this practice? Can you think of a better way of convincing someone to come and work on a ship?

_____
_____
_____
_____
_____
_____
_____
_____
_____
_____
_____
_____
_____
_____
_____

ENRICHMENT ACTIVITY

Throughout the remainder of this course, you are going to create your own gold rush short story. Every good story has interesting characters. Brainstorm 3-5 characters that you are going to write about in your gold rush story. What are your characters' names? Where are they from? What do they look like? What is each character's personality like? What are some unique characteristics about each character? Feel free to draw a picture of each of your characters. You will work on the setting and plot of your story in future lessons.

TO LEARN MORE

Look for this book at your local library:
Alaska and the Sea: A Survey of Alaska's Maritime History. By Antonson Mohr, Joan Anchorage: Office of History and Archaeology, Alaska Division of Parks, 1979. Summarizes Alaska's maritime history.

UNIT 7: SEA CAPTAINS, SCOUNDRELS AND NUNS

LESSON 28: SOAPY SMITH HEADS TO SKAGWAY

FACTS TO KNOW:

Soapy Smith – Jefferson Randolph Smith, nicknamed "Soapy," was a skilled criminal
Skagway – Southeastern Alaska city located on the northernmost point of the inside passage
Underworld – A term used to describe the world of organized criminals
Frank H. Reid – Skagway citizen known for giving his life to protect the Committee of 101 from Soapy Smith

COMPREHENSION QUESTIONS

1) Why was Soapy Smith drawn to the Klondike? _____

2) How did Soapy get his nickname? _____

3) How did Soapy Smith's telegraph office get gold from miners? _____

4) Why did a committee of Skagway residents decide to run Soapy out of town? _____

5) How did Soapy Smith die? Where is he buried? _____

DISCUSSION QUESTION

(Discuss this question with your teacher or write your answer in essay form below. Use additional paper if necessary.)

The Klondike Gold Rush inspired men and women from all over the world to come to Alaska. Consider all of the people that you have learned about who traveled to the Klondike during the gold rush period. What is your favorite story and why? Was this person seeking gold, adventure, fame or something else?

ENRICHMENT ACTIVITY

Now that you have brainstormed your characters, it is time to think about the setting of your story. Will your story take place on the Yukon River? Dawson City? Skagway? Cape Nome (which you will learn about in the next lesson)? Do you want to write a story that takes place in your fictional city from Lesson 22? Write a short paragraph to describe your setting. What does it look like? What does it smell like? What important landmarks are located there? You will work on the plot of your story during the next lessons.

TO LEARN MORE

Look for this book at your local library:
Southeast: Alaska's Panhandle, Alaska Geographic Society, Vol. 5, No. 2, 1978.

Soapy Smith
Word Search Puzzle
Find the words listed below

```
                                            U B
A C H I L K O O T T R A I L D K T           F G
E R E I D R M U C E V C O N M E N           E E
L U                             R D         Y D
U Y   Z X W V U F G T S G A     X S         X E
N A   Q D P H T R C F C M Q     X U         Y I
D W   U I           U A         E O         K A
E G   A A   K Q Z O L   T Y     H I         A H
R A   S P   G J Y H F   I P     E R         M G
W K   H Y   G J   E P   N A     N O         E N
O S   O Y   N N   J V   Y O     C T         H A
R C   U J   A T         O S     H O         C H
L Z   P L   G C P G K Z O L     M N         T S
D U   A S   S G B W Z H I T     E K         A P
B O   B I                       N D         K Z
I C   H N E I R B O S M I T H W G           J L
I I   D G S W V S G H K E U W R M           J P
U F                                         X X
U U G U N S L L R E M O H Y M P O S S       E
Q S G A S V B K H Z F R O B B E R S X       Y
```

MUTINY	SHANGHAIED	HOMER
QUASH	NOTORIOUS	GANG
HENCHMEN	UNDERWORLD	POSSE
SKAGWAY	CHILKOOT TRAIL	CON MEN
ROBBERS	SOAPY	SMITH
REID	KATCHEMAK	O'BRIEN

125

UNIT 7: SEA CAPTAINS, SCOUNDRELS AND NUNS

LESSON 29: MINERS STAMPEDE TO NOME

FACTS TO KNOW:

Three Lucky Swedes – The three men who discovered gold near Cape Nome in 1898 that spurred the Poor Man's Gold Rush
Cape Nome – A city on the northern shore of the Norton Sound in Alaska
Rex Beach – An American novelist and miner who wrote gold rush novels
Judge Arthur H. Noyes – A corrupt judge who was arrested for exploiting claimants in Nome

COMPREHENSION QUESTIONS

1) _____, _____ and _____ discovered gold that started the Nome gold rush. When did they make their discovery? How much gold did they find?
_____
_____

2) Why was the Nome gold rush known as the "Poor Man's Gold Rush"? _____
_____
_____

3) Was Nome known as a law-abiding town? Explain your answer. _____
_____
_____

4) What inspired novelist Rex Beach to write novels about the gold rush? What was the title of one of his famous gold rush novels? _____
_____
_____

5) How did the Poor Man's Gold Rush end? When? _____
_____
_____

DISCUSSION QUESTION

(Discuss this question with your teacher or write your answer in essay form below. Use additional paper if necessary.)

Why do you think there was so much crime in Nome? Think back to the different stories that you have read about in this chapter and previous chapters.

_____
_____
_____
_____
_____
_____
_____
_____
_____
_____
_____
_____
_____
_____
_____
_____
_____
_____

ENRICHMENT ACTIVITY

Now that you have brainstormed your characters and setting, it's time to think about the plot of your story. Brainstorm some ideas for your exciting gold rush story. Write down two or three possible story ideas. You will begin writing a rough draft of your story in the next lesson.

TO LEARN MORE

Read more about the Nome Gold Rush by visiting http://www.akhistorycourse.org/north-west-and-arctic/1897-1920-gold

UNIT 7: SEA CAPTAINS, SCOUNDRELS AND NUNS

LESSON 30: SISTERS OF PROVIDENCE HEAD TO NOME

FACTS TO KNOW:

Sisters of Providence – Four nuns who built the first hospital in Nome
Holy Cross Hospital – First hospital that opened in Nome on July 15, 1902
Fairbanks – The largest city in the interior region of Alaska
Anchorage – Alaska's largest city, located in southcentral Alaska

COMPREHENSION QUESTIONS

1) Why did the Sisters of Providence come to Nome? How did they travel to get there?
___
___
___
___

2) What kind of medical attention did the people of Nome receive before the sisters started their work there? ___
___
___
___

3) How did the sisters pay for the hospital? ___
___
___
___

4) Why did the Nome mission close in 1918? ___
___
___

5) What other areas of Alaska did the Sisters of Providence serve? ___
___
___
___

ENRICHMENT ACTIVITY

Using your brainstorming notes, characters, setting and plot, write a rough draft of your short story. Don't worry about grammar, spelling or punctuation on this draft. You will have time to edit your draft in the next lesson.

TO LEARN MORE

Read more about medicine in early Alaska by visiting http://www.akhistorycourse.org/americas-territory/alaskas-heritage/chapter-4-21-health-and-medicine

Most stampeders that made their way to Nome following the discovery of gold by the Three Lucky Swedes in the late 1890s had tents in the outfits they brought with them. With trees far and few between in the region, some adventurers relied on driftwood to help keep their shelters secure on windy days.

The information with this photograph said the miner shown here on the Nome beach in 1905 is Joseph Shaw, age 73.

MAP ACTIVITY

Identify the following cities on the map:
1) Nome
2) Fairbanks
3) Anchorage

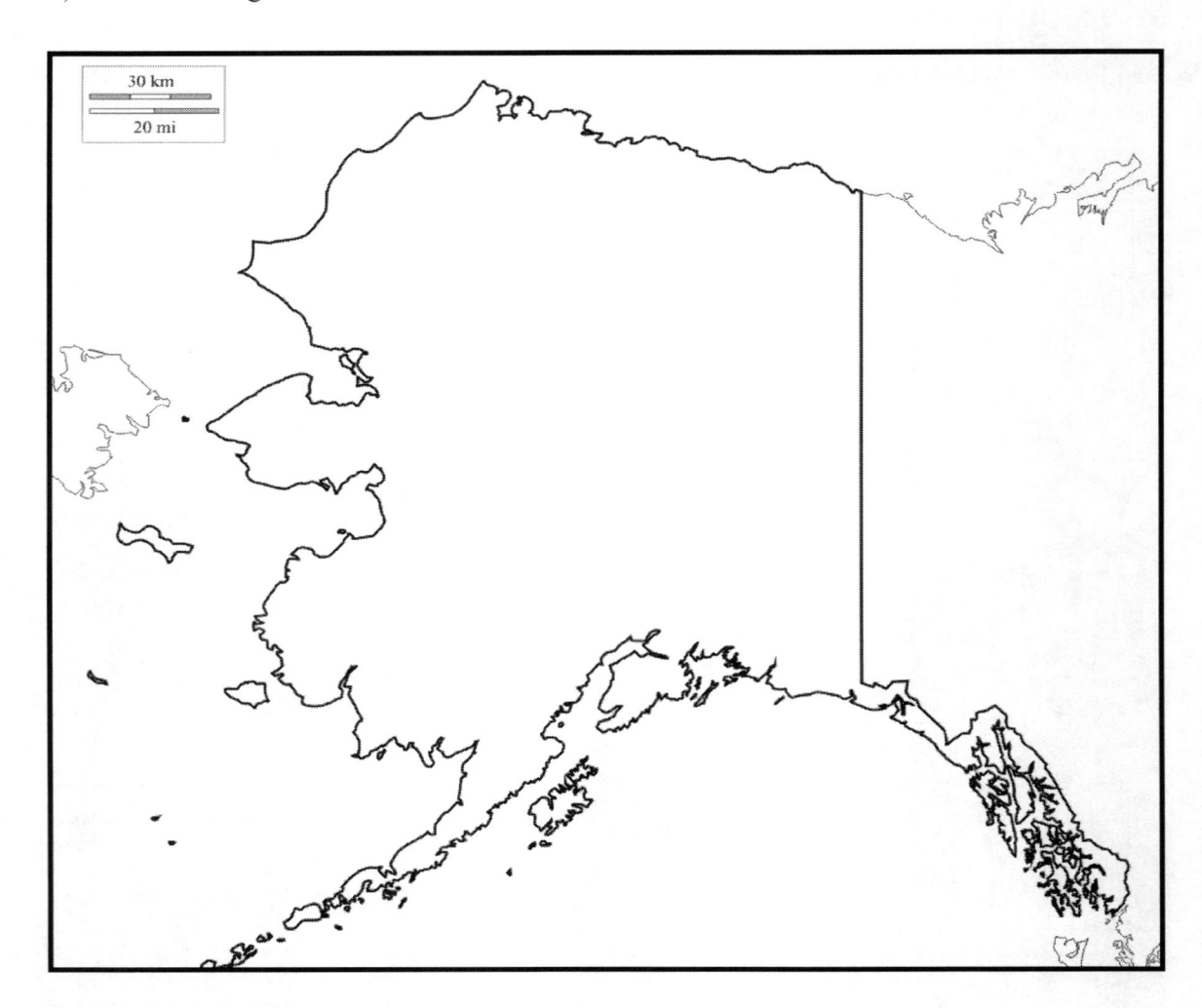

UNIT 8: GOLD RUSH IMPACTS NATIVES

LESSON 31: NATIVES AND THE RUSH FOR GOLD

FACTS TO KNOW:

Chilkats – Tlingit Indians along the Chilkat River and on Chilkat Peninsula
Chilkoots – Tlingit Indians along the Taku River
Southern Tutchone – Indian people of the Athabaskan-speaking group living mainly in the southern Yukon area of Canada

COMPREHENSION QUESTIONS

1) Summarize the editorial in the 1900 Dawson newspaper that voiced concern over the treatment of Alaska's indigenous peoples. _____
_____
_____
_____

2) How did the influx of white traders, prospectors and settlers change the Native's way of life? _____
_____
_____

3) In what ways did Native people help the miners? _____
_____
_____
_____

4) How did the Native people profit from the prospectors? _____
_____
_____
_____

5) How was the traditional Native way of life changed by missionaries? _____
_____
_____
_____

DISCUSSION QUESTION

(Discuss this question with your teacher or write your answer in essay form below. Use additional paper if necessary.)

How did many non-Natives view the indigenous people of Alaska?

_____
_____
_____
_____
_____
_____
_____
_____
_____
_____
_____
_____
_____
_____

ENRICHMENT ACTIVITIY

It's time to write the final draft of your gold rush short story. Read over your rough draft and correct any mistakes you made. Rewrite your corrected final draft. Share your final story with the class.

TO LEARN MORE

Look for this book at your local library:
Tlingit Stories, Maria Ackerman. Anchorage: Alaska Methodist University Press, 1975. A collection of legends from Southeast Alaska.

Tlingit Country Southeast

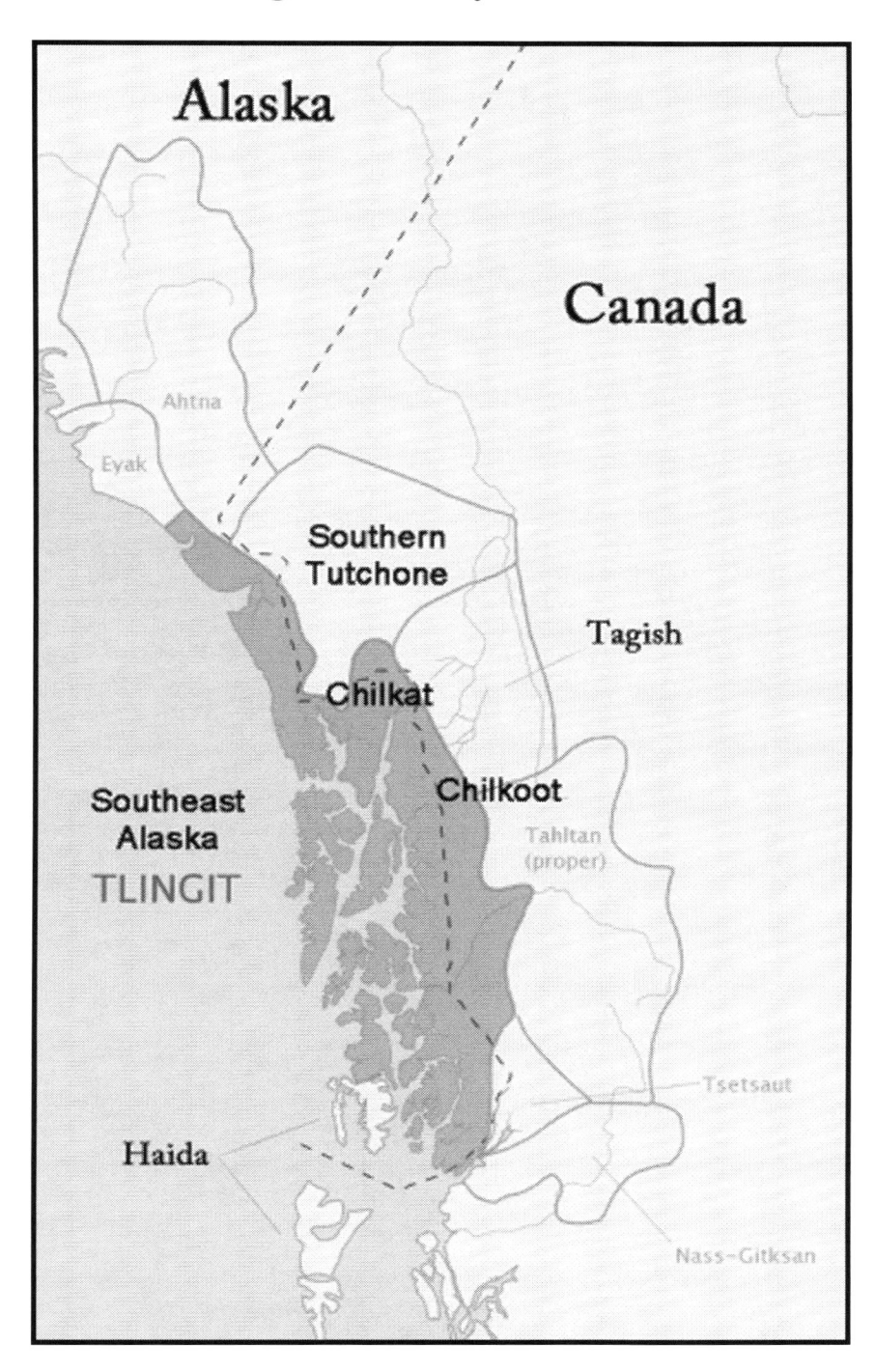

UNIT 8: GOLD RUSH IMPACTS NATIVES

LESSON 32: RICHEST NATIVE WOMAN IN THE NORTH

FACTS TO KNOW:

Mary Makrikoff – An Eskimo woman, also known as Sinrock Mary, who helped the U.S. government care for a reindeer herd in Nome
Sinrock – A settlement outside of Nome
Unalakleet – A village about 148 miles southeast of Nome on Norton Sound
Legacy – Something handed down from one generation to the next

COMPREHENSION QUESTIONS

1) According to Mary, in what ways was Nome different from St. Michael? What languages did Mary speak? _____
_____
_____
_____

2) How did Mary and her husband get into the reindeer herding business? _____
_____
_____
_____

3) Why did Sinrock Mary have to fight a legal battle to keep her reindeer herd?
_____
_____
_____
_____

4) How did she become the richest Native woman in the North? _____
_____
_____
_____

5) Why did Mary leave Nome in 1901? _____

DISCUSSION QUESTION

(Discuss this question with your teacher or write your answer in essay form below. Use additional paper if necessary.)

What was Reindeer Mary's legacy?

TO LEARN MORE

Look for this book at your local library:
The Eskimos and Aleuts. By Dumond, Don E., London: Thames and Hudson, 1979.

TIME TO REVIEW

Review Chapters 27-32 of your book before moving on to the Unit Review. See how many questions you can answer without looking at your book.

UNIT 7: SEA CAPTAINS, SCOUNDRELS AND NUNS
UNIT 8: GOLD RUSH IMPACTS NATIVES

REVIEW LESSONS 27-32

What do you remember about:

Captain Johnny O'Brien _____

Utopia _____

Shanghaied _____

Mutiny _____

Soapy Smith _____

Skagway _____

Underworld _____

Frank H. Reid _____

Three Lucky Swedes _____

Cape Nome _____

Rex Beach _____

Judge Arthur H. Noyes _____

Sisters of Providence _____

Holy Cross Hospital _____

Fairbanks _____

Anchorage _____

Chilkats _____

Chilkoots _____

Southern Tutchone _____

Mary Makrikoff _____

Sinrock _____

Unalakleet _____

Legacy _____

Fill in the blanks:

1) At age 16, _____ was _____ into working on a ship for six years. When he finally worked his way back to his home country of _____, he found out his parents had died.

2) A man traveling to Cook Inlet volunteered to nurse *Utopia* Captain _____ _____ back to health following an operation to remove his _____. That mystery man turned out to be none other than _____, better known to Alaskans as "Soapy."

3) The _____ Gang terrorized the people of _____ during the late 1890s. A committee of residents finally organized a group to run _____ and his gang out of town.

137

4) The _____ called a meeting on the dock on July 8, 1898, and placed _____ to guard the entrance.

5) Both _____ and _____ died from gunshot wounds as a result of a confrontration at the meeting of _____.

6) America's last big placer gold rush came in _____, when gold was discovered at _____ by three greenhorn Scandinavians.

7) Known as the "_____" the discovery of gold on _____'s beaches shortly after the Anvil Creek discovery meant that anyone could work the public property without staking or recording claims.

8) The influx of more than _____ prospectors working the gold-filled beaches of _____ brought with it the desperate need for _____ facilities. Before the arrival of the _____, the miners relied upon _____, often set their own broken bones and sometimes used _____ methods.

9) The _____ opened the doors to _____ hospital July 15, 1902.

10) At the time of the _____ purchase of Alaska, most _____ lived the traditional lifestyles of their ancestors, _____ for a living and governing themselves through ancient tribal systems. For some, the whites brought _____.

11) Born to an Inupiat Eskimo mother and a Russian trader father, _____ _____ was raised in _____. Her successful _____ business made her the _____ Native woman in the North.

12) When _____ died in 1948, she left a _____ of compassion and generosity. People still tell stories about how she shared her wealth the _____ way.

Alaska Natives and the Rush for Gold
Word Scramble
Please unscramble the words below

1. ednonisigu — First people to live in a place

2. neatnci — Very old, belonging to the very distant past

3. irtbe — A group of people that includes many families and relatives who have the same language, customs and beliefs

4. osiuetanc — Not easily letting go or giving up

5. neiws — A piece of tough fibrous tissue uniting muscle to bone, or bone to bone, that Natives used in sewing animal skin

6. ahlenouc — Small oil-rich fish

7. enrderei — Domesticated caribou used for food during Nome gold rush

8. qnpaiiu — Inupiat Eskimo language

9. roisnkc — Settlement outside of Nome

10. aaekunllte — Village where Reindeer Mary moved after winning the right to keep her reindeer herd

UNIT 7: SEA CAPTAINS, SCOUNDRELS AND NUNS
UNIT 8: GOLD RUSH IMPACTS NATIVES

UNIT TEST

Choose *three* of the following questions to answer in paragraph form. Use as much detail as possible to completely answer the question. Use extra paper in back of the book if needed.

1) Who was Captain Johnny O'Brien? How did he begin working on a ship at age 16? What happened when he became ill aboard his ship?

2) Describe Jefferson Randolph Smith. How did the people of Skagway stop him from terrorizing their city?

3) Why was the Nome Gold Rush called the "Poor Man's Gold Rush"?

4) Who were the Sisters of Providence? What did they do to serve the people of Nome?

5) In what ways did the influx of white prospectors, settlers and traders change the Native way of life in Alaska?

6) Who was the richest Native woman of the North? How did she make her riches? What legacy did she leave?

_____
_____
_____
_____
_____
_____
_____
_____
_____
_____
_____
_____
_____
_____
_____
_____

Aunt Phil's Trunk Volume One

UNIT 7: SEA CAPTAINS, SCOUNDRELS AND NUNS
UNIT 8: GOLD RUSH IMPACTS NATIVES

    Review Questions   _____ (possible 23 pts.)
    Fill-the-Blanks   _____ (possible 12 pts.)

Unit Test
  Essay 1
    Demonstrates understanding of the topic   _____ (possible 5 pts.)
    Answered the questions completely and accurately   _____ (possible 5 pts.)
    Composition is neat   _____ (possible 5 pts.)
    Grammar and Spelling   _____ (possible 5 pts.)

  Essay 2
    Demonstrates understanding of the topic   _____ (possible 5 pts.)
    Answered the questions completely and accurately   _____ (possible 5 pts.)
    Composition is neat   _____ (possible 5 pts.)
    Grammar and Spelling   _____ (possible 5 pts.)

  Essay 3
    Demonstrates understanding of the topic   _____ (possible 5 pts.)
    Answered the questions completely and accurately   _____ (possible 5 pts.)
    Composition is neat   _____ (possible 5 pts.)
    Grammar and Spelling   _____ (possible 5 pts.)

        Subtotal Points _____ **(possible 95 pts.)**

Extra Credit
  Word Puzzle   _____ (5 pt. per completed puzzle)
  Complete an Enrichment Activity   _____ (possible 5 pts.)
  Oral presentation   _____ (possible 10 pts.)

  Total Extra Credit   _____

        Total Unit Points _____

GRADE CHART

A   89-95+ points

B   80-88 points

C   72-79 points

D   64-71 points

EXTRA PAPER FOR LESSONS

EXTRA PAPER FOR LESSONS

EXTRA PAPER FOR LESSONS

EXTRA PAPER FOR LESSONS

EXTRA PAPER FOR LESSONS

EXTRA PAPER FOR LESSONS

EXTRA PAPER FOR LESSONS

EXTRA PAPER FOR LESSONS

EXTRA PAPER FOR LESSONS

EXTRA PAPER FOR LESSONS

EXTRA PAPER FOR LESSONS

Made in United States
Troutdale, OR
10/02/2023